WATERCOLOR

History and Technique

WINSLOW HOMER (Boston, Massachusetts 1836-1910 Prout's Neck, Maine).
Jumping Trout (detail). 1889. Watercolour. 315:492 mm. The Brooklyn
Museum, Dick S. Ramsay Fund, 1941.

WATERCOLOR
History and Technique

Walter Koschatzky

24 color plates
32 monochrome plates

McGRAW-HILL BOOK COMPANY
New York · Toronto

TRANSLATED FROM THE GERMAN

Das Aquarell

by Mary Whittall

ENGLISH TRANSLATION © 1970 THAMES AND HUDSON

© 1969 ANTON SCHROLL & CO, VIENNA

Printed in Italy and Switzerland. Bound in Holland.

ISBN 07-035369-8

Library of Congress Catalog Card Number: 72-87837

Contents

The Art of Watercolour

The concept of watercolour painting is simple and straightforward: the application of water-soluble colours to paper with a soft brush. The unique character of the medium rests in the fluid delicacy of the colours, subtle tonal variations without sharp linear definition, the gentle transitions and the transparency of the paintings. Watercolour offers the greatest possible freedom of painterly – as opposed to linear – expression, for it is essentially a medium of colour, not of line. Thus it has been most popular, and has made the most striking advances at certain specific periods in history when line has been almost totally out of favour as a creative medium. If we accept that there are no visible lines in nature, that to the eye an object consists of an area, or areas, of colour, then it follows that drawn lines and outlines are the product of an intellectualizing process.

Watercolour is the painterly medium *par excellence*, and a preliminary definition of its essential nature is implied by the contrast between the linear approach – intellectual in origin and thus imposing a barrier between the spectator and nature – and the painterly approach, rooted in visual perception and ranging in effect from the realistic to the visionary. If we pursue these polarities, it is not hard to relate them to the alternating rhythm of deduction and induction which beats throughout the entire history of western thought: drawing and line seek to define truth, the goal of all deduction; reality, the source of all induction, yields itself more readily to painterly methods. The contrast between the ideal outline drawings of Flaxman, the embodiment of Winckelmann's theories, or the delicate linearism of the Nazarenes on one hand, and the colourful works of the *plein air* school, naturalists and realists on the other is enough to illustrate this: as a broad generalization it may be said that the former embody an intellectual approach, concerned to define and illustrate the working of the divine order and the platonic 'idea' behind the objects portrayed, while the latter are informed by a spontaneous love for the beauty of the visible world which finds expression through more painterly techniques. It is noteworthy that watercolour, more than any other artistic medium, has, at least until the twentieth century, been chiefly and continuously concerned with the visible world: with nature, landscape and atmosphere.

To enumerate the subjects in which watercolour excels is to acknowledge that it is more suited to recreating the world in general impressions than by precise representation. The painting technique has some bearing on this of course, but the determining factor is the brilliance of colour which has a life of its own; the act whereby the colour is applied to the paper is still visible in the finished work and exercises a unique charm on the eye of the spectator.

When painting with watercolours there are three basic ways of combining two colours. The first is to wait for a wash or brush-stroke of one colour to dry before painting another colour over it: yellow painted over blue in this way will give green, but the combination of the two colours occurs only where one stroke overlays the other; where they are not overlaid, each will mark the paper with its own colour. Thus even a single brush-stroke drawn across another can result in three different colours on the paper. The second method is to combine two colours, already dissolved in water, on the palette before application; again, a mixture of yellow and blue will produce green. The third method is to apply a second colour while the first is still wet on the paper, so that the combination results from the two colours running into each other; this can have the most delightful results, producing shading of the softest kind. As early as 1410 Cennino Cennini mentions this 'wet' method in his treatise on painting, the *Libro dell' Arte* (Chapter 31): 'By this means your shading will resemble gently drifting smoke.'

The potential range of the effects that can be obtained even from the simplest combination of two colours is already surprisingly rich. Fundamentally watercolour painting employs the three primary colours: yellow, red and blue, and also black. Simple combination of any two primary colours will result in what are called the secondary colours: blue and red combine to make purple or violet, red and yellow make orange, and all nuances of green can be obtained by mixing blue and yellow in varying proportions. Tertiary colours are combinations of all three primaries in unequal proportions (equal proportions would produce a neutral grey): thus a preponderance of red, if mixed with blue and yellow (i.e. green), gives brown, and so on. It is not my intention at this point to give a systematic exposition of all the possible combinations, only to indicate the almost miraculous way in which the realm of colour can be extended. Exploration

I ANTHONY VAN DYCK (Antwerp 1599–1641 London).
Hilly landscape with trees. Grey, blue and green wash, pen in brown ink. 228:330 mm. The Devonshire collection, Chatsworth. Inv. 1003. Vey 306.
In the last decade of his life, Van Dyck painted a group of watercolours of English landscapes. Up to 1634 the pen played the dominant role, but in this work the scene is sketched out entirely by the brush and the pen is used only afterwards, to go over some of the outlines.

II

of colour is, after all, the meaning and purpose of all painting, and of watercolour in a quite particular sense, because of the incomparable range of nuances it can achieve. Whether the colours are mixed on the palette or overlaid on the paper, the resultant hue will depend on the degree of saturation of the primary colours, and even if it were possible to limit the degrees of saturation to three: dense, medium and thin, the variety of hues that could be obtained from the three primary colours alone would by vast. In fact, of course, there are no such clearly defined degrees and the number of hues and nuances available to the painter is infinite.

There is another sense in which colours may be said to combine: in addition to the relationship between colours laid one above the other, a relationship also exists between colours laid beside one another. It may be one of mere tolerance or of mutual enhancement, its effect pleasant or unpleasant – colours may contrast, harmonize, arouse tensions, or simply remain indifferent to each other. The exploitation of these relationships is one of the fundamental principles of painting. There is also a chemical tolerance between pigments which the artist must understand, but which need not be discussed here. We are concerned, not with precisely definable physical stimuli, but solely with an aesthetic reaction to the appearance of colour as used by the artist to creat that formal unit which we call a work of art. In the context of artistic creation, what colour 'does' is of a psychological nature; it releases immediate and spontaneous emotions in the spectator. In *Concerning the Spiritual in Art*, Kandinsky writes:

> The superficial impression of colour [may] develop into an experience ... the second result of looking at colours: *their psychological effect*. They produce a correspondent spiritual vibration ... Men of sensitivity are like good, much-played violins which vibrate at each touch of the bow. Colour directly influences the soul. Colour is the keyboard, the eyes are the hammers, the soul is the piano with many strings. The artist is the hand that plays, touching one key or another purposively, to create vibrations in the soul.

To put it more simply, some colours seem aggressive, others peaceful; some colours stir the spectator to action, others calm him. This polarity of

II PAUL CÉZANNE (Aix-en-Provence 1839–1906).
Still-life: Apples with Glass and Bottle. Watercolour over drawing. 450:597 mm. Courtauld Institute of Art, London.
The painting dates from the period 1904–06. Its strong but simple construction clearly displays the basic forms of sphere, cone and cylinder. 'To paint from nature does not mean copying the object, but realizing the impressions of colours ... I have perhaps come closest to this end in still-life.'

response demonstrates the principle of active and passive colours which are often described as warm and cold – terms chosen for their associations, since the 'warmest' colours are fiery oranges and reds, the 'coldest' icy greenish blues. Perhaps the most important formative element in painting is the use of this tension between warm and cold colours to create an illusion of space on a flat surface. Warm colours advance, cold colours recede, active reds surge towards the onlooker from the surface of the picture while passive blues retreat. As the eye moves over the surface it absorbs this interplay of colour forces, which is one of the fundamental experiences of art appreciation; the colour nuances stimulate the spirit as well as the eye, they excite, they calm and their 'properties' arouse varying sensations in quick succession. In this respect watercolours create more intense stimuli than any other kind of painting because they are small, often very subtle, and the transparency of their tints allows particularly delicate nuances.

The great sensitivity of watercolours is primarily due to the immediacy and spontaneity the medium allows the artist, since the actual technique is of the very simplest order. It is often said that the essence of the medium lies in the speed of execution it affords, an assertion which cloaks a number of serious misapprehensions, but which is incontrovertible in two respects. Firstly, in the sensitive hand of an artist, a watercolour brush, with its capacity for gentle modulation, is an incomparable seismograph of the most delicate impulses, even of the stirrings of the unconscious. Though akin to drawing in this, watercolour is perhaps pre-eminent in its ability to reflect the hand, the personality of the artist. In this context speed is not related to the technical simplicity which made possible the glut of watercolours painted by *dilettanti* over the last century, but to the immediacy with which an impression or a spontaneous 'inspiration' can be expressed in visual form. Secondly, the simplicity dictated by the technical conditions, the speed with which watercolours dry, the easily portable materials – a pad, brushes and a few colours – make watercolour the ideal medium for the traveller. For centuries artists have been going out into the wide world to record its beauties, its splendours and its chance phenomena. This made them prone to look on watercolour as nothing more than a medium in which to make quick, coloured sketches from life, on the basis of which the large-scale 'true' work of art in oils could be 'composed' by idealists, or 'recreated' by realists in the studio. The inferior status of watercolour moved professional and amateur watercolourists in eighteenth-century England to form societies to promote the medium in defiance of academic opinion and to defend the purity of genuine watercolour against the impurity of body colours.

The accumulation of meanings can sometimes make nonsense of a term, and in the case of watercolour it is particularly essential to use the word with precision so as to avoid the confusion arising from careless usage. A good example of such ambiguity occurs in Lothar Brieger's *Das Aquarell* (Berlin 1923) which, as a result of the dearth of authoritative studies, became the standard work on the subject. Of the 216 illustrated examples approximately 90 are not watercolours in the strict sense of the word at all, but coloured drawings, brush drawings or gouaches. Some limits must be set on the use of the word if it is to be meaningful, but certain factors should be taken into consideration. Except in England, the use of body colour for some details of watercolours is a generally accepted rule. There is also a body of monochromatic works – such as brush in bistre or sepia, in indian ink, in blue, grey or neutral-coloured inks – which do not merely constitute an important preliminary stage of watercolour painting, but can be considered as genuine watercolours in their own right; they bear the hallmarks of transparency and application of colour in washes, and their general effect is, by and large, the same. Like any other technical term, the word watercolour must be used with a certain amount of latitude and individual works should be judged according to their merits. Not every drawing in indian ink wash can in practice be called a watercolour, while a single brush-stroke of body colour, which in any case can often be thinned down to the point of transparency, is not in itself enough justification for excluding a work from the category.

Nevertheless, in the terminological confusion that has arisen, certain criteria should be stated. Such criteria cannot be purely technical; it is not enough to define watercolour as a product of colours dissolved in water, it must also be defined as an artistic medium. Material and technical properties cannot be separated from the formal, creative elements. The paints, the wet brush and paper, the seismographic immediacy, the transparency and the effects of atmosphere and space must all be comprehended as means whereby a quite specific artistic process takes place which also involves a specific attitude to the world of appearances – a process in which transparency becomes the symbol of the intangible and spiritual and body colours the expression of material reality.

The Technique of Watercolour Painting

While the medium known as watercolour owes its name to the fact that it employs pigments dissolved in water, it is not identical with all painting in which water is the vehicle but only one quite specific variety. The use of water-soluble colours dates from the earliest days of human history, for once pigments had been extracted from mineral, animal or plant sources, dried and ground to powder, water was the most obvious solvent. From the rise of the earliest civilizations to the invention of oil-painting, with the exception only of a few kinds of tempera all painting throughout the world involved the use of water-soluble colours. In Assyrian mural paintings and in the Egyptian Books of the Dead, in China and later Japan and Korea on fans, paper lanterns, screens and scroll paintings, in Etruscan tombs, in early Christian catacombs and in Byzantine manuscripts, the vehicle for the transference of the colour to the surface was always water. These colours were used for linear outline, for priming a surface, for colouring and touching up drawings and for illuminating incunabula. But none of these uses can be called watercolour.

From the technical standpoint, watercolour painting can be defined as the application of transparent layers of pigment, ground to the very finest consistency, to pale, virtually always white paper using water as the vehicle. Paper is the only material which has the properties necessary for true watercolour; ivory and even silk were once frequently used but, in fifteenth-century Europe, the manufacture of paper in large quantities for the first time was as important a factor in the development of watercolour as it was for engraving and drawing.

It is not enough simply to dissolve powdered pigments in water and apply them to the surface of the paper with a brush; as soon as the water dries the colour will become powder once more, to be shaken or brushed off the paper. A binding agent, usually gum arabic or certain kinds of lime, is also necessary; this must be soluble, so that it can be taken up with the pigment on a wet brush. Then, when the water dries, the gum hardens and fixes the colour on the paper. Nowadays it is no longer necessary for artists to prepare their own colours; all sorts of shades can be bought ready for use, in cake or in tube form and it would be superfluous to spend time on the technical minutiae of mixing colours, important though they once were.

Naturally the relative proportions of pigment and water in solution determine the saturation and thus the strength of each colour, as well as the density of each layer of paint on the paper. A lot of water will result in pale, light tones, a more concentrated solution in more saturated colours. But a high degree of saturation is not to be confused with opacity, for transparent watercolours and opaque watercolours are two fundamentally different things. True watercolour is painting with transparent colours; painting with opaque water-soluble colours, or body colours is called gouache.

It has often been said that the distinction between watercolour and gouache which was so fanatically upheld in England in the eighteenth and nineteenth centuries is out of date – certainly German and French artists have never taken very much notice of it. It is, however, not merely a matter of distinguishing between two related categories, but between two totally different genres. The very expressions 'watercolour' and 'body colour' contain the essence of the distinction. In some respects gouache or body colour resembles oil-painting since the first stage in a gouache is to cover the paper with a ground on which to build up the painting layer by layer and stroke by stroke. The artist begins by painting the dark areas, overlays them with lighter hues and finishes with white highlights; the result is a dense fabric of forms and colours, often resembling *impasto*, which covers the entire surface of the paper. The opaque white with which body colours are mixed usually creates a flat, chalky effect, though sometimes the very strength of the colours can give the painting a sharp luminosity. Body colour is thus better suited to rendering the corporeal substance of details for, when used in large areas, it can easily become dull and monotonous.

Watercolour, too, depends for its effect on the particular physical properties of pigments laid on in successive layers. But they are different properties from those of gouache, for each layer of watercolour wash remains transparent. It is not so much the use of water as solvent which gives the medium its name (for body colours use the same vehicle) as the transparency it gives, the transparency of clean water. As a result, the paper always remains visible and its texture can be an important element in the completed work. But even more important, light is reflected not only from the uppermost surface but, after penetrating every layer of paint, from the paper itself as well – hence the use of white paper, on which the layers of paint lie like sheets of coloured glass.

Thus while the painter in gouache proceeds from dark to light, the process is reversed in watercolour. The highlights are provided by areas of the white paper which are left unpainted. The palest hues are painted first, then progressively stronger ones, with the darkest shadows last of all. The very essence of this technique derives from the transparency of the materials: each layer of paint remains visible through the layers above it but at the same time allows new colours to appear. The inexhaustible variety of nuances which can be achieved in this way is what gives watercolour painting its unique charm.

The History of Watercolour Painting

The history of watercolour is not a steady, unbroken chain. Since the beginning of the sixteenth century the medium has come to the fore only at certain times when it evidently met a specific inner need, and the important stages in its history are clearly definable and separated. This fact demolishes Brieger's theory that watercolour has played a constant role as a preliminary stage, a kind of practice ground for artists before going on to greater things.

In the last decade of the fifteenth century Albrecht Dürer produced a series of unique works in watercolour, a medium which he then, strangely, abandoned as he turned to other problems. It is equally strange that his contemporaries and successors, who adopted so many of his ideas and techniques, did not also take up watercolour; there are a number of works in body colours by Albrecht Altdorfer, some coloured pen-and-ink drawings, but that is virtually all. The use of water-soluble pigments in the portraiture of Lucas Cranach the Elder and Hans Holbein the Younger, was entirely in keeping with the new immediacy with which artists of that period viewed individual physiognomy and the visible world, but many of these works were drawings overlaid with body colour. Nevertheless they mark an important historical stage between Dürer and the next high point of watercolour proper, which came in the seventeenth century with the landscapes of Anthony van Dyck and the advent of monochromatic watercolour landscape in the work of Adam Elsheimer, Claude Lorrain and Nicolas Poussin.

During the sixteenth and seventeenth centuries a realistic outlook on the world had slowly evolved in the northern part of the Low Countries which embraced the immediate environment as well as the Italian South of every artist's dreams. Dutch watercolour came into its own in *vedute* and scenes of everyday life and, quite suddenly, artists like Adriaen van Ostade produced watercolours that were accepted as finished works in themselves. In Germany and Austria the practice of decorating albums (*Stammbücher*) in watercolour gave the medium opportunities to develop, though many of the examples are of a low standard artistically. But it was in England, where the ideals of freedom and natural simplicity prepared the ground for a new appreciation of nature, that all the lines of development can be seen to converge with an intensifying concentration like the rays of the sun passing through a lens. In the eighteenth century foreign travel for pleasure was widely undertaken for the first time, and every traveller seems to have carried his brushes and watercolours with him, producing a torrent of *vedute* and landscapes from both at home and abroad. At the same time changes in the structure of society produced amateur activity of a kind that had never been seen before. Two divergent trends soon emerged in landscape painting, one realist, the other imaginative, and both rose to such heights that there was little else on the contemporary artistic scene to be compared with them. France was infected with an Anglomania which introduced not only philosophies and political ideals but also the art of painting in watercolours and the new view of landscape which the medium revealed. There is a very real bridge reaching from Richard Parkes Bonington as far as Monet and from him to North America. In the nineteenth century, when French painting led the world, nearly every great French artist from Eugène Delacroix to Paul Cézanne, painted some of his best work in watercolour. The impressionists, too, in their struggle to master the problems of light, used watercolour to great effect, and the tradition which originated in England is still actively and persuasively carried on.

Schools of watercolourists also arose in Germany, Austria and Switzerland, which raised the art of landscape painting to a high level. Swiss artists, evidently under direct English influences, took to painting Alpine scenery at a very early date. Although generally motivated by a romantic animism unknown in England and hardly known in France, Germanic artists developed a realist mastery of the subject matter. Eighteenth-century Vienna, strictly academic in its orientation, achieved an abrupt and unexpected height in a minor art form: the miniatures of Heinrich Füger, in which technical skill and sensitivity combine to give these portraits of noble ladies, painted on ivory, a unique charm. Watercolourists of great ability succeeded each other throughout the nineteenth century: Peter Fendi, Carl Schindler, Thomas Ender and Rudolf Alt, the genre painters of the Düsseldorf Academy, the romantic realists of the

Munich School, chief among them Karl Rottmann, and above all the Berlin School. This procession reached a magnificent climax in the work of Karl Blechen and came to a no less glorious end with Adolf Menzel, who developed a highly personal technique combining gouache and watercolour with brilliant results.

The dawn of the twentieth century brought a temporary halt, probably as a reaction against the misuse of overworked techniques. The refined delicacy of tone which had prevailed up to then was not likely to appeal to the expressionists, though the members at *Die Brücke* (founded in Dresden in 1905) and *Der Blaue Reiter* (founded in Munich in 1911) soon made the surprising discovery that watercolour lent itself very well to their new styles. Ernst Ludwig Kirchner, Karl Schmidt-Rottluff and August Macke constructed pictures with a spontaneous and exuberant use of aggressive local colour, giving the medium an expressive power which was to reach its highest level in the work of Lovis Corinth, Oskar Kokoschka and Emil Nolde. Franz Marc almost always used body colours, but Kandinsky laid the foundation for abstract art in watercolour, as in other media, and, since the Second World War, artists the world over have exploited the freshness of watercolour, the modulations made possible by its transparency. They are bringing to fruition the process which began with Cézanne: diverting the medium from portrait and landscape and putting it to new uses, treating its illusory surfaces flooded with coloured light as a plane for free, poetic creation.

This brief history of watercolour painting over the centuries shows that it has been most frequently used in landscapes and portrait miniatures. Albrecht Dürer, the first artist to explore the possibilities of watercolour, was led to this means of expression by the deeper appreciation of nature that marked the transition from the Middle Ages to the Renaissance. He learned the technique as a young man, during the travels he undertook on completing his apprenticeship in Nuremberg. 'When I had served my term, my father sent me away and I remained abroad for four years, until my father summoned me again. And as I set out in 1490 after Easter, so I returned in 1494 after Whitsun.' It may have been immediately after this that he painted his first watercolour landscape in the country outside Nuremberg.

In the early days of printing it was customary to colour engravings in emulation of illuminated manuscripts; the latter were rare and costly and printing allowed illustrated texts to be produced cheaply and in great numbers, but the printers nevertheless clung to the convention of colouring the woodcut illustrations. The illuminators of manuscripts used opaque tempera because it allowed the initials and miniatures to stand out on the parchment page, but in printing it was not necessary or desirable to hide the lines of the engraving with colour: transparent watercolour was found to be the appropriate medium for colouring woodcuts. It was in taking an everyday ancillary technique and turning it into an artistic medium in its own right, in his sudden recognition of the potentialities that lay in the colour alone, without the support of the printed drawing, that Dürer's genius asserted itself. This use of an established technique in an entirely new way (not least in recognizing the role that areas of unpainted paper could play in a picture) gives Dürer the right to be called the father of the art of watercolour.

The awakening interest in nature at the beginning of the modern era proved to be a decisive step into a new world and watercolour played no small part in the subsequent progress. Landscape was regarded as the essential embodiment of nature, and thus the only proper object of art, and watercolour was the ideal medium to make visible the intangibility of atmosphere. The landscape painter Max Schmidt wrote in 1870:

In landscape paintings, it is in innumerable cases the air which our eye perceives before all else. Its insubstantiality makes it fundamentally different from the corporeal earth and its phenomena. It is our image of infinity and forms the strongest possible contrast to the fixed delimitations and tangibility of the forms of the earth's crust. The air and its modulations contain the most splendid and enthralling natural impressions that the human soul is capable of comprehending. The innermost essence of the artistic mind can never be fully captured in words ... but in general it can be said that the infinite range of our moods, from innocent gaiety to the deepest melancholy, finds a mode of expression in the living atmosphere about our globe, or more correctly, that the soul finds correspondences to all its varying moods in the variations of the atmosphere.

Above all other media watercolour possesses the capacity to unite intangibility and the perception of reality, the experience of beauty and the most profound introspection. It is this that gives it a permanent place in the history of the arts.

The Watercolours of Albrecht Dürer

Albrecht Dürer (1471–1528) used water-soluble colours in about sixty-five of the roughly one thousand studies and sketches that survive today; amongst them are thirty-one works which can be called watercolours in the very strictest sense. These unusual works, almost all of which are landscapes, were painted during the space of about twelve years around the turn of the fifteenth century. They are extraordinary not merely in the context of Dürer's work but in the context of art history as a whole. The technique of painting with watercolours had been known from the very earliest times, and suitable paper had existed for several centuries, but these works are something quite new and without any kind of precedent. In them Dürer incorporated all the essentials of the art of watercolour as set out in the first chapter: painting with the brush and with transparent, water-borne colours giving objects pictorial substance and formal function solely by mixing the colours, applying them in overlapping washes and allowing them to merge while wet. And what is even more astonishing is that not only did Dürer himself suddenly stop working in the medium, but nobody else took it up throughout almost the whole of the rest of the sixteenth century.

Scholars have naturally tried to find explanations for the abrupt appearance of the watercolour in Dürer's work, but none of the various hypotheses advanced – the situation at that particular moment in time, the stage reached in stylistic evolution, artistic necessity – are substantial enough. Remarkably, there is not a single mention of the use of watercolour as an independent medium in all Dürer's writings, which are full of his opinions on a wide range of artistic topics; usually he returned repeatedly to subjects that he thought important, seeking new words with which to explain his theories and methods of work.

It is also significant that Dürer never once refers to landscape painting in his writings. The obvious conclusion is that he also viewed landscape as neither a significant element in his work nor even as a separate artistic genre. This certainly seems to be confirmed by looking at his drawings, nearly all of which are of figure subjects. Landscapes are rare and generally appear in an ancillary role, specifically as background studies for biblical subjects. The few examples of landscape as a subject in its own right all belong to one or other of two groups: the first dates from the period around 1500, and the second, which is much smaller, from the time of Dürer's journey to the Netherlands in 1520–21. The connection between Dürer's travels and his landscapes is an important one, for the earlier and much larger group, which includes the watercolours was also inspired by impressions of travel, particularly of the first journey to Venice in 1494–95. The watercolours testify to a transitory interest in the landscape he saw about him as he travelled, as well as to a previous, and more abiding interest in the familiar countryside of his homeland.

A letter Dürer wrote to Willibald Pirckheimer from Venice on 7 February 1506 contains the first mention of a previous visit to the city: 'the thing which pleased me so greatly eleven years ago pleases me no longer. And if I had not seen it for myself, I would not have believed it from anybody else.' This establishes that he must have been in Venice at some time in 1494–95 but the ingenious research that has sought to discover just what 'the thing' was that had lost its power to please has been without success. Did he perhaps find that the spontaneous response to the landscape that he had experienced on his first journey was no longer the same? If this were true it would help to explain some features of his subsequent artistic development, including his sudden discontinuing of the use of watercolour. In any case, the significant fact remains the relationship between Dürer's initial interest in landscape and his first journey to Italy, particularly, so far as we are concerned, because it sheds light on the series of watercolours.

Further confirmation of the early dating of his watercolours is provided by the engraving *Nemesis* (also known as *Das große Glück*), in which an allegorical figure hovers above a mountainous landscape with a riverside town, identifiable as Chiuso in the South Tyrol. Dürer must therefore have journeyed through the South Tyrol some time before 1501–02, the date of the engraving. The lofty angle from which the town is viewed is a common element in his early watercolours of scenes near Nuremberg, such as the *Wire-drawing Mill*, probably painted before his first journey in 1494. The naive, almost primitive technique of the *Wire-drawing Mill* has frequently been remarked on and Hans Tietze went so far as to call it 'childish and indigent'; even the colouring, in greens, browns and pale blue, is flat and

III ALBRECHT DÜRER (Nuremberg 1471–1528).
Arco. Watercolour and body colour. 221:221 mm. Autograph inscription in the top right-hand corner. *Fenedier klawsen* [Venetian mountain pass]. Louvre, Paris. Winkler 94.
On his way to and from Italy in 1494–95, Dürer painted a series of watercolours in which he progressed from the status of a beginner to that of a master in the medium. In this painting he uses subtle nuances of colour, particularly warm and cool greens, and combines meticulous refinement of detail with imposing construction, luminous transparency with physical solidity, and finally strictest realism with the truth that only the greatest artists can convey.

fenedier klaussen AD

III

IV

undistinguished. But if one compares the picture to the slightly earlier *Christ Child with Globe* in the Albertina in Vienna, for example, which the artist worked with the point of the brush in tempera on parchment in a completely traditional fashion, then it must be admitted that the view of the open landscape, the realism and the technique, however uncertain, of the *Wire-drawing Mill* represents a truly astonishing advance. For all its shortcomings this work marks the beginning of landscape as an independent genre.

What Dürer could do with the wet brush at a very early stage in his career is best illustrated by the monochrome *Madonna in a Gothic Niche* (W 142), which, whatever its precise date, makes it plain that Dürer had already mastered the essentials of watercolour painting by about 1495. Before his abilities could blossom in mature works a specific impetus was necessary: the recognition of landscape as a sufficient subject in itself for a painting. This must have dawned upon him between his return from Basle and Strasbourg and his departure for Italy in 1494. These two prerequisites, the technique and the vision, now combined with a third element: experience of Alpine scenery, but even this would not perhaps have been enough to enable him to scale the ultimate heights but for his contact with the great art of Venice and, above all, with the landscape backgrounds in the paintings of Giovanni Bellini.

Dürer's watercolours have been subjected to serious study by generations of scholars, but a number of points still lack absolute clarification. They fall into four distinct groups: a) four early works painted in Nuremberg; b) fifteen landscapes of the Tyrol and the South Tyrol, presumably painted on his first journey to Venice in 1494–1495; c) five studies of quarries; d) seven late Nuremberg pieces. Even so, between the topographical evidence on the one hand and questions of style on the other, it was a long time before even this grouping was generally accepted and much remains obscure. While Dürer's route across the Alps and the location of many of his subjects have been established by individual scholars, questions of dating are still open to considerable disagreement. One of the problems lies in the failure, as yet, to trace the stylistic evolution of the works with complete certainty.

The order in which the South Tyrol watercolour landscapes were executed is one of the major problems of Dürer studies. In view of the decisive experience of his first stay in Venice, it is reasonable to assume that his work

IV ALBRECHT DÜRER (Nuremberg 1471–1528).
Pond in the Woods. Watercolour and body colour. 262:374 mm. Monogram by another hand. British Museum, London. Winkler 114.
Painted in the countryside outside Nuremberg between 1495 and 1497, this is above all an evocation of atmosphere: clouds, air, colours in sunlight. The work is informed by a new attitude towards nature and in it, Dürer achieves full artistic maturity.

would have been more conventional on his journey south in the autumn of 1494 than on his return in the spring of 1495, and consequently that, to take two important examples, the view of Innsbruck (*pl. 2*) dates from the outward journey and *Alpine Landscape* (*pl. 4*) from the return. The former, now in the Albertina, is a pure watercolour executed in the style of a miniature; ever since Moriz Thausing's study based on Dürer's works in the Albertina it has been regarded as one of the key works for the understanding of Dürer's landscapes. For a long time the inscribed title 'Isprug' led to the mistaken belief that the subject was a town with a similar name in north Germany. After this problem had been settled the dating became the chief ground for controversy. The only certain historical fact is that the tower of the arsenal is depicted as it was before reconstruction in 1496. The watercolour scrupulously reproduces every topographical detail and must be the first accurate view of a town, painted for its own sake, in the modern era (prospects like this were to give rise to the artistically far more modest genre of the *veduta*). The fortified town is seen, from some distance away and almost from ground level, across the waters of the Inn. The angle was probably chosen for the sake of the reflection on the water but it marks a new stage in Dürer's artistic development, for he abandons the more traditional bird's-eye view, even at the sacrifice of one of Innsbruck's most striking characteristics, the way in which it is closely encircled and sheltered by mountains. The division of the composition into parallel horizontal bands – the river in the foreground, the town across the centre and the mountains in the background – betrays the young Dürer's still rudimentary conception of space. The empty foreground, which lacks any *repoussoir* feature, the insubstantiality of the buildings and the absence of concentration on any one central motif are other signs of artistic immaturity.

If we turn from this picture to the Alpine landscape which Dürer called *Welsch pirg* (*pl. 4*) a decisive difference is immediately apparent. The foreground and middle ground are painted with broad summary strokes and a full brush in a wide range of greens; the dynamic forms pile up in a diagonal sweep of colour towards the imposing, forest-cloaked mountain in the background, the obvious centre of the artist's attention. The contrast between the plastic detail of the background and the broad, summary planes of the foreground gives the scene a unique attraction very different from the naive freshness and charming simplicity of the Innsbruck picture. The concentration on the mountain rising up between the foreground masses at the end of the valley creates a depth which stretches back as far as the high mountain in the extreme distance. Essential to the colouring and mood is a delicate pink, a reflection of the rising or setting sun, which emanates from the clouds in the background, and spreads very faintly across the whole of the foreground. Even if we take into account that part of this watercolour's fresh impression stems from its sketchy, half-finished condition, it none the less clearly represents a decisive turning-point in Dürer's attitude to landscape in two respects – recognition of scenic grandeur and perception of atmospheric phenomena. The splendour of a scene in nature, something that cannot be defined solely in terms of scale or topography, is here expressed by the very intangibility of its individual elements.

Among Dürer's other Alpine scenes his painting of the small hill town of Arco (*pl. III*) stands out. An extraordinary luminosity emanates from this work, which is painted in cool shades of the loveliest greyish-green watercolour, with the more solid details – in body colour. In the top right-hand corner Dürer wrote '*fenedier klawsen*', indicating that the subject was a mountain pass somewhere on his road to or from Venice, but it was a long time before it was positively identified as a view of the castle of Arco which dominates the valley of the river Sarca to the north of Lake Garda. The dating was another matter on which there were for a long time conflicting opinions although it is now accepted that the work dates from Dürer's return journey in 1495. The formal character of the scene is largely determined by its format which is more or less square. The rocks which frame the foreground direct the eye in towards the centre, where undulating ground, dotted with trees and vines, rises to the small walled town. Beyond, more trees climb steeply up one side of the hill which, flanked on the other side by a rocky precipice and crowned by the castle, dominates the landscape. The olive grove, the mulberry trees, the vineyard and the sparkling river combine with the even light which extends over the whole scene to create an incomparable impression of a southern landscape penetrating into the mountains. A photograph taken from Dürer's vantage point would show a massive range of mountains in the background, so there can be no doubt that he left them out deliberately to prevent his central feature being diminished, just as he chose to ignore the mountains in his view of Innsbruck. But the fuller exercise of the technique also employed in *Alpine Landscape* displays some important advances in the artist's mastery of landscape since painting the city on the Inn: the majesty of the composition; the articulation of the elements so as to create depth and breadth; the concentration on a single motif and on a diagonal perspective which leads the eye deeper into the picture; all engender a necessary elemental power in the view of Arco, and the omission of the mountainous background shows that Dürer did not feel himself the slave of topographical accuracy. There is something crystalline about this lucid, painterly composition, which strengthens its aloof coolness.

If all these characteristics could be described as 'classic', the *Pond in the Woods* (*pl. IV*) must be called 'romantic'. This watercolour, painted after the return to Nuremberg in 1495, shows plainly that Dürer's relationship to nature had deepened. The brightness of the atmosphere, gently hinted at in *Alpine Landscape*, here becomes an essential element of the composition. A notable feature in the development of Dürer's watercolour landscapes is the way in which man-made features progressively recede in importance: in the view of Innsbruck the town itself is the subject; the castle at Arco is part of an imposing landscape; *Alpine Landscape* depicts the sublime grandeur of the mountains, beside which the works of men appear insignificant; and finally, in this painting of the pond, the appearance of a natural feature is subject enough in itself. The dark blue of the water fades as it recedes into the distance, flanked by the multiple unity of the trees on the right and the disjointed group of bare trunks on the left. Impressive streaks of cloud hang over the scene, and the foreground is devoted to grass, drawn with loving care. The contrast between the green of the grass and the blue of the water draws attention to the limitless expanse which stretches away, without any horizontal interruption, into infinity. A decisive change is apparent in the colouring as well as the composition. Whereas in his earliest works Dürer juxtaposed local colours, filling in outlined areas with opaque colour, he has now learned, by means of transparent washes, modulation of tones and veiling of spatial depths, to recreate the working of nature in a landscape. Neither heroic nor idyllic, the scene is not heightened by the artist's imagination; its natural individuality is eloquent enough. The date of this work is uncertain but it is generally put between 1495 and 1497; the foreground shows a new interest in graphic and linear elements, which certainly justifies a relatively late dating, for these were shortly to become of great importance in Dürer's development. Once again, there is no denying that it is the incomplete, sketchy character which gives the work an unintentional modernity. Dürer succeeded in enclosing in this small scene a world that was new both to him and to his age; the emotional awareness it displays was not to be surpassed. For Dürer himself the work marks the end of a chapter, for soon afterwards he embarked on a study of physical proportions, hoping to discover universal laws which, he believed, determined the true dimensions of all beauty. In purely material terms line drawing, and not watercolour, was the suitable means to this end. It is nonetheless curious that Dürer seems never again to have felt drawn to work in watercolour, even when his search for proportion had long ago led him to the discovery that striving for certain knowledge often proves more limiting than uncertain groping towards a truth that lies beyond reality.

Although they are the product of just one phase of his artistic career, Dürer's watercolours occupy a commanding and unparalleled position in the history of the medium. This naturally raises the question of just what part watercolour played in Dürer's creative method. There is an obvious connection between his use of watercolour and his experience of landscape for although at all stages in his career he used drawings to remind himself of purely topographical features, there seem to have been certain quite specific sensations which he found himself unable to record in any other medium. This practice was something more than a casual collecting of subject material. The appearance of an actual locality in his engraving of *Nemesis* – the village of Chiuso in the South Tyrol – indicates that when he first set eyes on it and either sketched it or committed it to memory he must have sensed in the physical character of the spot a significance which later seemed appropriate to his allegory of capricious fate (the figure of relentless Nemesis has taken on something of the unpredictable quality of Fortuna), perhaps symbolizing the defencelessness of Man's work in the path of elemental natural forces. Although we have no record of his views on the depiction of landscape among his writings, Dürer's frequent expositions of his creative processes are so general in their application that they can probably be taken to embrace landscape as well as other subjects. He writes that it is essential to the creative process that the artist

> should fill his spirit with much copying of things seen. This is not an end in itself but is converted into artistic skill, which germinates, grows, and bears fruit after its kind. The secret store gathered in the heart is made manifest in the work, the new creation which the artist fashions in his heart in the form of a specific object. That is the reason why an experienced artist does not need models for every painting, for he can draw on the store he has gathered over a long period. The practice will benefit his work, but very few realize its value.

Although it is hard for us to understand why, Dürer cannot have shared our high opinion of his watercolours; they nevertheless form part of the 'secret store of his heart' on which he drew for his work. His watercolour landscapes document the evolution of his experience of nature, and it was probably by his efforts to record atmospheric moods that he learned the elementary significance of the effect of light. This accumulation of experience can be seen to bear fruit in at least one of his major works, the *Adoration of the Trinity*, also known as the Landauer Altarpiece, now in the Kunsthistorisches Museum in Vienna, in which the light is an active element as the sun rises on the new, eternal day after the Last Judgment. It is not merely by chance that the strip of scenery painted at the bottom of the picture is strongly reminiscent of Lake Garda and its surroundings; it must have been the memory of his experiences in that region, fortified perhaps by watercolour studies, that enabled Dürer to add the finishing touch to the altarpiece, which he completed in 1511.

Less can be said about the briefness of the period in which Dürer worked in watercolour; presumably it was long enough for him to gather as much as he needed for his 'secret store', or else he would have continued to use the medium. A general conclusion about the series of watercolour landscapes is suggested by Dürer's lifelong interest in portraiture: that his chief concern was not so much with the individual appearance of his subject (whether human or topographical) as with the exploration of its fundamental 'complexion' or temperament. 'Thus the external measure of every kind of person serves to reveal their nature, whether it be fiery, airy, watery or earthy', that is, whether they are choleric, sanguine, phlegmatic or melancholy in temperament. In his own view and in that of his contemporaries this was to reveal in some measure the cosmic foundations of human nature. He may well have believed that, in expressing the 'external measure' of nature in his watercolours, he was, simultaneously, revealing the essential 'complexion' of the landscape.

Dürer's Wash Drawings and Gouaches

Thirty-four of the studies and sketches in water-soluble colours which remain are not strictly speaking watercolours but they are, nonetheless, interesting. They can be divided into three fundamentally different groups.

The first group comprises pen-and-ink drawings painted over or, in Dürer's own phrase, 'touched up' with watercolour. Dürer himself called them 'half colours' (*halbe Färblein*) and their purpose seems to have been to make the sketches clearer to himself when he came to use them in a more 'finished' work, and more attractive to the patron who had commissioned it (for example, the sketch for the *Adoration of the Trinity*, which he drew for Martin Landauer in 1508). An explicit reference to their use in this way occurs in a note Dürer wrote on 16 March 1521: 'I have drawn a view in half colours for Tomasin and he will have his house painted on the basis of it.' The use of very thin, transparent wash occurs throughout Dürer's œuvre, from the *Madonna with Musical Angels* (Winkler 35), one of his major early works, to the very end of his career, in, for instance, the *Annunciation* of 1526 (W 894). One of the outstanding works in this group is the *Madonna with the Many Animals* of c. 1503, in the Albertina. The delicate and varied greens of the plants, meadows, trees and distant hills are interwoven with passages of the most delicate pink in the shadows, the house, the rock, the flowers and even in the corona of the star, and finally with an equally delicate blue in the parrot, the cushion, the pond, the sea and the sky. The very simplest means are used to create a chromatic composition which, for all its delicacy, brings out an austere greatness and balance in the construction of the peaceful, reflective scene. The 'half colour' is an important artistic medium in Dürer's hand, but it is not, strictly speaking, watercolour.

The second group includes the penetratingly observed studies of plants and animals, of which the two best known must be *The Young Hare* (W 248) and the *Large Piece of Turf* (W 346), both in the Albertina. The faithfulness with which Dürer reproduces the smallest detail has been justly praised time and again. It is important, not merely because it demonstrates the completely controlled technique, without which he could not have accomplished these works, admirable in itself, but even more because it is symptomatic of his wish to reveal the Creator in even the smallest and least significant of His works. As Tietze said, all these studies have one thing in common: the seriousness, the veneration, the fanaticism with which the artist immerses himself in his subject. For Dürer's generation the presence of God everywhere in the universe was not just a vague Neo-Platonic truism but a reality which could be verified by painstaking examination of the smallest details of the physical world. There is a dramatic tension in Dürer's work, which flows from the ever-changing relationship between the desire to comprehend and the incomprehensible, between recognition and the unrecognizable; from visionary insight and sensitivity to nature he moved towards an understanding of the laws of harmony and proportion until he finally perceived the unfathomable mystery of creation and the 'miraculous gift' of artistic inspiration.

A particularly important element in this process is the belief that it is possible to comprehend the absolute beauty that underlies the randomness of the ordinary and the particular by careful observation of their details, 'for truly art is concealed in nature, it belongs to whoever can draw it out.' There is no substitute for nature as the foundation on which the artist must build, 'therefore never take it into your head that you could make something better than it is in nature, for the power of nature is the gift of God, its creator.'

Nevertheless, the concept of reality in these minutely observed brush drawings, from the incomparable studies of the *Jousting Helmet* (W 177, Paris), the *Soldier on Horseback* (W 176, Albertina), and the traditional Nuremberg costumes (W 224–8) to the *Birds Wing* and the *Hooded Crow* (W 614 and 615, Albertina) of 1512, is not the same as in the landscapes. They are also distinguished from the other studies by their technique, for they are worked over in very dense body colour applied with the point of a hard brush. Using white paper, Dürer often begins with a faint outline drawing and then paints a tinted ground of transparent watercolour on which he builds his form with strokes of body colour, using ever greater density to create both shadow and highlight. This group therefore cannot truly be called watercolours either, for their most characteristic elements stem from the linear brushwork in body colour. The subjects he depicted in this medium, apparently insignificant in themselves are astonishingly timeless: a hare, a patch of meadow grass, common wild flowers, the rather repulsive snout of an ox. It is a choice paralleled in Goethe's lines:

> *Geb Gott Dir Lieb' zu Deinem Pantoffel,*
> *Ehr' jede krüpplige Kartoffel,*
> *Erkenne jedes Dings Gestalt*
> *Und fühle, wie die ganze Welt*
> *Der große Himmel zusammenhält.*

('God grant you a love for your slipper; honour every misshapen potato, acknowledge the form of every object and feel how the whole world rests in the hand of heaven.')

The third group comprises monochrome and bichrome brush drawings, again not really watercolours; indeed, in some of their most interesting and characteristic aspects they are the exact opposite of watercolour. It was during the first weeks of his second stay in Venice in 1505 that Dürer made a major innovation in his already legendary brush technique. His first acquaintance with *carta turcha*, green or blue paper, led him to use coloured grounds on which the unprecedented linear precision, which is his hallmark in every medium from copper engraving to gouache, could appear to maximum effect. The colour of the paper forms the medium value. An outline of the subject is drawn with the brush in a dark colour and parallel strokes then model and shade the body. Finally the lights are painted in the same manner in white, with the brush kept as sharp as a pen, only more supple in its strokes. The network of lines, reinforcing each other, creates depths, shadows and an infinite subtlety of form, and yet its basic constituents are the simplest imaginable. Dürer went on using this technique for many years, from the painstakingly detailed studies for the *Feast of the Rose Garlands* (e.g. W 385 etc.), like the *Hands of an Apostle* (W 461, also known as *Praying Hands*) to the *Portrait of an Old Man of Ninety-three* (W 788) whom he encountered in Antwerp in 1520–21. The discovery of this almost graphic brush technique in 1505–06 brought an end to the fluid watercolour painting of the preceding years. The change from one technique to the other was a dramatic one, and evidently occurred during his preparatory work for the *Feast of the Rose Garlands*. A study for the Pope's robe in this painting (W 401, Albertina) is a pure watercolour, painted with a full brush; the magnificent embroidered cloak of purple and gold which falls from the shoulders of the kneeling figure is at once transparently fine and superbly material. This study, one of Dürer's most remarkable works, is in all probability his last watercolour; all the other studies for the *Feast of the Rose Garlands* are in his new-found, graphic brush technique.

1 VITTORE PISANO, CALLED PISANELLO [?] (Verona 1397–1455)
Three studies of coursing. Watercolour on parchment. 255:171 mm. Louvre, Paris. Inv. 2568.
E. Sindona attributes this to Pisanello, Degenhart and Fossi to the Lombard School. It probably dates from before 1450 and is one of the earliest examples of observed nature and also of the new technique of painting in watercolours.

2 ALBRECHT DÜRER (Nuremberg 1471–1528)
Innsbruck from the North. Watercolour. 127:187 mm. Albertina, Vienna. Inv. 3056.
This dates from Dürer's first journey to Italy in 1494–95 and is the earliest example of his use of transparent watercolours.

3 (After) JOHN WHITE (active, late sixteenth century)
English Sailors in a Skirmish with Eskimo. Pen and brown ink and watercolour. 390:285 mm. British Museum, London. Inv. 78, f. 12v.
Probably a facsimile of a watercolour depicting an incident during Frobisher's first voyage of exploration in 1577. It is not known whether White's original was done at second hand or whether he actually accompanied the expedition and painted it from life; he did, however, sail with Raleigh's first expedition to Virginia in 1584, as explained on p. 40.

4 ALBRECHT DÜRER
Alpine Landscape (Welsch pirg). Watercolour. 210:312 mm. Ashmolean Museum, Oxford.
According to Winkler, this dates from Dürer's return journey from Italy, in the spring of 1495; according to Tietze, from his second journey to Italy in 1507. The broad delineation of the foreground is contrasted with the careful detailing of the mountain behind.

5 NICOLAS POUSSIN (Villers 1594–1665 Rome)
The Ponte Molle, near Rome. Bistre wash and pen drawing. 197:371 mm. École des Beaux-Arts, Paris.
One of Poussin's most vivid and yet monumental studies of nature, dating from shortly before, or immediately after his stay in Paris, 1640–42. His technique of leaving the highlights blank was taken up by later watercolourists.

1

2

3

4

5

6

7

10,11 ►

8

9

12

6 CLAUDE GELÉE, LE LORRAIN (Chamagne 1600–82 Rome)
Landscape with Trees at Eventide. Bistre wash. 222:328 mm. Boymans-Van Beuningen Museum, Rotterdam. Inv. F. I. 12.
The beauty of the Roman Campagna was an inexhaustible source of inspiration to Claude. His superb brush technique enabled him to capture the effect of light in the depths and expanses of natural scenery.

7 NICOLAES BERCHEM (Haarlem 1620–83 Amsterdam)
Peasant and Cattle at a Ford. 1655. Black chalk, pen and ink and watercolour. 285:445 mm. Albertina, Vienna. Inv. 9805.
Berchem, one of the most skilled of the Dutch italianists, was in Rome from 1642 to 1655. His treatment of light had an important influence on the English watercolourists.

8 ALEXANDER COZENS (St Petersburg? *c.* 1717–86 London)
The Cloud. Grey and black wash. 216:318 mm. Armide Oppé collection, London.
The most famous of Cozen's drawings, a perfect blend of imagination and realism.

9 JOHN SELL COTMAN (Norwich 1782–1842 London)
Chirk Aqueduct. Watercolour. 327:232 mm. Victoria and Albert Museum, London. Inv. 115–1892.
The man-made construction dominates its landscape setting. The painting is a study of light, shadow and reflection.

10 THOMAS GIRTIN (London 1775–1802)
The Mouth of the Seine. Watercolour. 118:248 mm. City Art Gallery, Birmingham.
Girtin spent the last two years of his life in France, where he attained a freedom of technique far in advance of his age. The sparkling lights in the foreground were painted with a dry brush; the large masses in the background merge into each other. Nearness and distance are represented with equal skill; the brightness and shimmer of the water are incomparable.

11 JAMES MILLER (active London, late eighteenth century)
Cheyne Walk, Chelsea. Watercolour. 410:632 mm. Victoria and Albert Museum, London. Inv. 731–1893.
Painted around 1776, by a member of the early English school of watercolourists, typical in its attempt to combine a topographical view with a romantic mood.

12 JOSEPH MALLORD WILLIAM TURNER (London 1775–1851)
Grand Canal; Sunset 1839. Watercolour. 219:318 mm. British Museum, London.
After 1801 Turner made a final break with all traditions and his views of towns became visionary impressions, in which the mood is the essential subject.

Watercolour Painting in the Sixteenth and Seventeenth Centuries

The overwhelming influence which Dürer exercised on his contemporaries, the effect of his major accomplishments in woodcut and engraving, his graphic style, his coloured grounds, his brush and pen techniques, lingered on for generations. It is all the more strange therefore that his watercolours were virtually ignored by his contemporaries and successors alike. Circumstances would seem to have been particularly favourable for the development of the medium: there existed a strong trend towards painterly, rather than graphic, expression and a special interest in the visible world, as opposed to the Platonic 'ideal' world. These were notably the characteristics of the group of artists known rather loosely as the Danube School, and it is really astonishing that none of the major artists among its numbers worked in watercolour, apart from the occasional colouring of sketches and drawings. Their love of nature was very much an instinctive emotional response, of the kind expressed by Conrad Celtis: '*Mich entzücken die Quellen und die grünen Hügel, die kühlen Ufer des murmelnden Baches, die dichtbelaubten, schattigen Wälder und die üppigen Gefilde.*' ('They enrapture me, springs and green hills, cool banks of murmuring streams, dense-leaved, shady woods and lush meadowland.') This was the spirit that was abroad in the early years of the sixteenth century among artists from Regensburg to Vienna, in Bavaria, the Tyrol and Salzburg.

The outcome was a South German and Austrian school of landscape painting which reached its peak in the panel paintings, drawings and engravings of Albrecht Altdorfer (*c.* 1480–1538). Compared with Dürer's watercolours, which are cooler, more considered and more concerned with topography, Altdorfer's work is more animated, expressive and always imbued with a pervasive mood. Altdorfer's sensitivity to atmosphere might seem to make watercolour the ideal medium for him, but he never worked in it. He did however leave four landscape drawings in water-soluble pigments: *Alpine Landscape with Church* (Rotterdam), *Landscape with a Woodcutter* (Berlin), *Alpine Landscape at sunset* (Erlangen) and *Landscape with Castle and Courtyard* (Dresden), as well as some sketches and his contributions to Jörg Kölderer's *Triumph of Emperor Maximilian* (Vienna), all of which combine luminous chromatic force with the most sensitive response to atmosphere. However, all these are not watercolours but pen-and-ink drawings painted over with body colour, and technically they correspond in every way to contemporary book illumination. The other leading member of the Danube School, Wolf Huber (1480/85–1553) whose responsiveness to atmosphere has perhaps never been equalled, is believed to have been acquainted with Dürer's watercolour landscapes, but he too never used the medium. The general stagnation in all the arts during the relentless struggles of the Reformation and Counter-reformation, the iconoclasm which took hold of the regions dominated by Protestantism and the civil wars that subsequently raged all over Germany and Austria may explain why the potential of watercolour which Dürer had revealed was not further explored. Long after his death Dürer remained an isolated figure in the history of watercolour painting. Nevertheless during the next two centuries a web of connecting threads was spun in preparation for the next major resurgence of the medium in England.

In Italy the whole spirit of the age was opposed to any vital appreciation of landscape. Particularly after the Sack of Rome in 1527, which resulted in the dispersal of Roman artists all over Italy, there arose a decided and increasingly powerful movement towards academicism, accompanied by a trend towards anti-rational, transcendental speculation and the occult; watercolour, whose essence is the immediacy of visual experience and spontaneous recording of colour and atmosphere, could find no place in this atmosphere. A whole series of mannerist theoreticians in the first half of the sixteenth century proclaimed the divinity of the artist and the supremacy of his inspiration; Lommazo even went so far as to say: 'It is the duty of art to correct the errors made by nature.' The supposed conflict between spirit and matter, truth and reality, the divine and the mundane dictated a theoretical order of importance among the various possible subjects of art and landscape came at the very bottom (a position it continued to occupy in some schools of academic theory until well into the nineteenth century). Taken to its ultimate conclusion, this kind of mannerist reasoning was capable of inferring that a copy of a work of art was more worthy than a work painted directly from nature, because artistic genius had supposedly played a smaller role in the latter than in the former.

The mundane virtues of watercolour came to be more highly prized in a context far removed from the intellectual climate of Italy. England, like the other leading maritime nations such as Spain and the Netherlands, had entered an age of discovery and colonization. Natural scientists accompanying the explorers returned with a wealth of information on the flora and fauna, geology, geography and anthropology of the new worlds, and it was not long before the practical value was recognized of taking artists along as well to make visual records of the new discoveries; the speed and simplicity of watercolour painting made it the ideal medium for this purpose. The

39

first artist to go to the New World seems to have been Jacques le Moyne (c. 1530–1588) who took part in the French expedition to Florida of 1564. He spent the rest of his life in England, and the studies he painted on the voyage encouraged Sir Walter Raleigh to take a 'draughtsman-surveyor', John White (c. 1540? – c. 1600) with him when he set out on the first of his North American expeditions in 1584. White's duties were probably much the same as those of Thomas Bavin who had accompanied Sir Humphrey Gilbert to New England in 1582 and was charged with the 'graphic record' of coasts and countries, harbours and settlements, unusual happenings, flora and fauna, the native inhabitants, their dress and way of life. Upon White's return to England in 1586 his pictures at once reached a wide public through the engravings of the Fleming, Theodore de Bry. A large number of the original paintings, which are of immense historical value, are preserved in the British Museum, including an album that, for all it is inscribed 'Originall draughts by Mr John White', may be a copy of White's notebook (see *pl. 3*). Sir Hans Sloane, in a letter written in 1709 to the Abbé Bignon, recounts that he had had such a copy made, firstly because he had been unable to purchase the original, and secondly – and herein lies its interest for us – because the original was almost worn out from handling by young painters who had used it in learning their craft. Clearly the intervening generations had recognized that watercolour is the ideal medium for the traveller. It is interesting that the increasing use of watercolour owed so much to its purely practical convenience; that alone would have accounted for the future pre-eminence of the medium in England.

During the sixteenth century a very special appreciation of the real world evolved in Holland, or, to be precise, in the northern provinces of the Netherlands. This owed nothing to contemporary Italian art, despite the former close contact between the two countries, and the Italian-influenced art of the Romanists and the ideal landscapes of the mannerists meant little to a generation of energetic and successful merchants and traders. There was an increasing demand for art to represent the Dutch environment, prompted not least by a certain individualistic pride in that environment. In every age, art performs a function in the society that supports it. A well-ordered bourgeois society, whose serious involvement with the practical affairs of life was mixed with a certain cheerful complacency about its own achievements, could not possibly want the same things from art as, say, the court of Spain; the Protestant view and the artistic policy of the Counter-reformation laid down by the Council of Trent were poles apart. For all the variety of personal styles and the schools associated with different towns – Amsterdam, Delft, Haarlem – Dutch art of the late sixteenth and early seventeenth centuries is characterized by a constant and universal interest in the appearance of the real world. At a deeper level this is one of the fruits of Dutch thought that contributed so much to the rise of the natural sciences and led to the philosophy of Baruch Spinoza (1632–1677), whose attempt to reconcile the dualism of idea and reality was an important stage in the development of pantheism and the reappraisal of the worth of actual existence.

The effects of the political independence from Spain won by the United Provinces in 1581 were far-reaching, for they ushered in a period of great economic prosperity that lasted until about the end of the Thirty Years' War in 1648. Soon after that the supremacy of England at sea and of France on land began to alter the situation, but by then realism had found its place in art all over Europe and pantheism had brought about a new relationship between man and nature and a new awareness of landscape.

The Dutch School and its Influence

From about 1620 Haarlem became a leading centre of landscape painting, with the depiction of scenes in the town's immediate vicinity by the Ruysdael family and perhaps also by Jan Wynants. An even more momentous event was the appearance of the first works in watercolour to be represented as complete works in their own right (until then water-colour studies were described as 'archetypes' for oil-paintings). These scenes of peasant life by Adriaen van Ostade (1610–84) were complete paintings in every respect, though they are all rather similar and their stereotyped atmosphere of cheery well-being becomes somewhat monotonous.

Life in seventeenth-century Holland is more vividly evoked in the watercolours of Hendrik Avercamp (1585–1663). His fresh, softly-shaded scenes of skaters taking a holiday on the frozen canals are painted in a manner that combines refinement and freedom. Nicolaes Berchem's work is more lively still, notice-ably that of a painter of the next generation (he lived from 1620 to 1683), although the ruins and con-ventional shepherds of his landscapes show that he was deeply immersed in the world of Italian art. He reached his peak about 1660, in imaginary southern landscapes, with flocks and streams and a general atmosphere of warmth and sunshine, depicted with a light, free hand (*pl. 7*).

Watercolour painting made an important step for-ward in the landscapes of Anthony van Dyck (1599–1641), who came not from the Protestant northern Netherlands but from Catholic Flanders, from the full-blown High Baroque world of Rubens. Van Dyck's watercolours are a small and isolated part of his tremendous output. Strictly speaking there are only four of them: *A Farmyard* (British Museum), *Trees with a Harbour in the Background* (Barber Insti-tute, Birmingham) and two landscapes at Chatsworth (see *pl. I*), but they have justly been described as the *incunabula* of English watercolour painting. They probably date from the last decade of the artist's life, after his move to London in 1632, but the absolute freedom of Van Dyck's brushwork had been apparent from an early stage, even in ink-and-wash studies painted before he went to Italy in 1622. The land-scapes he saw by Campagnola and Titian in Venice, by the Carracci and Domenichino in Bologna, by Tassi and above all by Paul Bril in Rome, were a challenge to him. Experience, technical freedom and sensitivity combined in a completely new vision of limitless distance, which is reproduced in his water-colours with a meticulous refinement of detail ('glorious pedantry', Panofsky calls it), yet with a suggestion of dissolving horizons. This late style, made possible by the immense changes that had taken place in Van Dyck's lifetime and the strength he gained from the religious outlook of the early Baroque, was helped, in addition, by his experience of Italian art and by the realism of Dutch landscape painting. Van Dyck's watercolours had an important influence on the future development of English land-scape painting; in particular their deliberately un-finished effect – none of them actually fill the sheet of paper – was an influential innovation.

Among the large number of German artists whose work illustrates the general and far-reaching influ-ence of the Dutch masters, the Moravian Georg Flegel (1563–1638) gives an astonishing example of the perfection to which realism could attain in a series of 110 watercolours (Berlin-Dahlem), still-life compositions in which plants, fruits and small ani-mals are depicted with the most scrupulous regard for detail. Flegel worked with Lukas Valckenborch in Austria before moving to Frankfurt, which be-came his second home. The other main genre to develop from realism was the topographical view, and here Dutch influences are discernible in the work of Matthäus Merian the Elder (1593–1650), who also settled in Frankfurt, in 1624. Among Merian's pupils there was the Bohemian Wenceslaus Hollar (1607–77), who was employed by the Earl of Arundel in 1636 to accompany him and record his travels – the tradition that started with John White was taking root! Hollar lived in London from 1652 until his death and his amazingly large output made a sub-stantial contribution to the appreciation of landscape and views by a wider public.

While most of Europe north of the Alps was devastated between 1618 and 1648 by one of the longest and most destructive wars in history, Rome, long recovered from the effects of the Sack of 1527, was entering a new and splendid era. The artistic potentialities of the city's ruins, pregnant symbols of the transience of earthly glory, had already been recognized in the latter part of the preceding century. To the receptive eye they merged with the surround-ing Campagna to form the 'ideal' harmonious land-scape and thus, in the afterglow of history, the natural scenery earned attention for its own sake. A kind of 'romance of ruins' had been propagated by Maerten van Heemskerck (1498–1574) and by Jan Gossaert and Jan van Scorel before him, and now a new generation of northern artists followed their example by studying in Rome, among them Paul Bril (1554–1626) whose gentle, elegiac vision and sensitive response to nature added a new quality to landscape painting.

Historically at least, the most important figure among these artists was the German, Adam Elsheimer (1578–1610), who, having already succumbed to the influence of Dutch landscape painters, went to Rome in 1600 and spent the rest of his short life there. His *œuvre* comprises fifty paintings, all of a small format, and some eighty drawings, none of them in watercolour, but including a series of thirty-three brush drawings in gouache, now dispersed between the Kupferstichkabinett in Berlin-Dahlem, the Albertina and other collections. Painted on a coloured ground, they bear a curious resemblance to *grisailles*, and represent one of the important stages in the progress towards the emergence of watercolour as an independent medium. The ostensible subjects are still biblical, but the landscape settings mark an advance, the significance of which can hardly be overestimated. Elsheimer wielded his brush in a completely new fashion: the application of the monochrome wash is fluid and expansive; the highlights are left bare; gradations of shadow are achieved by repeated overpainting; groups of trees are drawn together in great masses. It is Elsheimer who deserves the credit for the discovery of the Campagna as the 'ideal' landscape; the seventeenth-century German chronicler Joachim von Sandrart records that Elsheimer would spend half a day, even a whole day, in studying a fine tree, in order to recreate every detail of its appearance when he returned to his studio. In this 'ideal' landscape Elsheimer created a subject that was to preoccupy art for centuries to come.

The foundations laid by the German were built on by a young Frenchman, Claude Gellée (1600–82), called 'le Lorrain' after his homeland. He went to Rome while still a boy and soon discovered his talent while painting landscape backgrounds in the workshop of Agostino Tassi. In 1625 he returned to France, intending to settle down, but after only two years, during which he continued to mature as an artist, he was drawn irresistibly back to Rome where he spent the rest of his life. Joachim von Sandrart, who arrived in Rome in 1629, became associated with the colony of artists to which Sacchi, Domenichino, Pietro da Cortona, Bernini and Poussin also belonged. He also became a very close friend of Claude, and we owe a great deal of our knowledge of the Frenchman to Sandrart's biographical writings. It is significant to learn that, until about 1630 painting from nature was still regarded in Italy as something disreputable. The idea still prevailed of a higher artistic truth that was opposed to the debased reality of nature; in order to become the subject of a work of art, every visible phenomenon of nature had to be ennobled by the human spirit and painted, not on the spot, but only after it had been perfected in the artist's memory. Sandrart writes that Claude

sought to approach nature in every way he could, going out into the fields before dawn and staying until night, so as to be able to represent dawn, sunrise and sunset in a truly natural manner, and when he had well observed one or the other, he at once tempered his paints to match what he saw, ran home and used them on the work in progress with far greater naturalness than any had done before him.

The day came when Claude saw Sandrart, at the Tivoli waterfalls, actually painting in the open air, something which Sandrart had learned from the Dutch, to whom it was a matter of course, and was astonished to realize that his friend was painting from life. After that he too began to paint from nature. His contacts with the Dutch colony in the Via Margutta may also have helped him to see the artistic virtues of realism but there was never any likelihood that Claude might become a realist himself; on the contrary, he was the great practitioner of that 'ideal' landscape which academies were later to discredit through endless and insipid imitation. Nonetheless, Claude began to make studies directly from nature, not employing watercolour as such but a technique without which watercolour painting might not have managed to evolve any further. These studies in bistre, no less than those of his compatriot Nicolas Poussin (1594–1665), whose lively temperament introduced quite different but equally valuable elements, deserve to be called monochromatic watercolours. (*pls. 5 and 6*)

Claude's achievement was to raise the drawing of landscape to a totally new category of art. Plentiful evidence is to be found in his *Liber Veritatis*, a volume of nearly two hundred pen-and-wash copies of his works, drawn by his own hand, which he made, according to Filippo Baldinucci, to safeguard his *invenzioni*, his original ideas, against piracy. This book became immensely influential; sold by his family it was brought in the middle of the eighteenth century from Paris to England, where the Duke of Devonshire bought it around 1770; it is now in the British Museum. The work became widely known as the result of a facsimile edition (1774–77) by Richard Earlom, which is a masterly illustration of the advances made by English printers in mezzotint, etching and crayon engraving. It would of course be an oversimplification to ascribe Claude's enormous popularity in England to this publication alone – it is based rather on a deep affinity – but whatever the reason, by the end of the eighteenth century two-thirds of his entire *œuvre* was to be found in England, where it contributed to the enthusiasm for nature that was then in vogue. It also opened the eyes of practically a whole generation of English artists, encouraging them to emulate Claude's technique in creating their own personal vision of the outdoor world.

Watercolour in England

Eighteenth-century England saw an extraordinary flowering of watercolour painting. Developing out of the long-standing native tradition, the medium steadily rose in popularity and technical achievement during the course of the century, reached dramatic heights in the final decade and finally spread English influence to the continent. Yet all this ultimately derives from a single factor – the particular suitability of watercolour for expressing a new attitude towards landscape, a new concept of nature.

A whole series of artists have been dubbed 'fathers' of the English watercolour landscape, but this plural paternity only shows that they all started from the same philosophical premise – that propounded around 1700 by Anthony Ashley Cooper, third Earl of Shaftesbury. Starting from the proposition of his tutor, John Locke, that the primary means of any perception is through the senses, Shaftesbury's system went much further in promoting feeling to an unprecedented position as an absolute moral category. As soon as 'moral sensualism', for example pleasure at in the sight of a landscape, is conceived to be a direct cognizance of the divine, the way is open to pantheism. In this context worship of nature and of scenic beauty becomes something utterly different from the enjoyment of nature and from finding refreshment or recreation in the open air; nature becomes the new foundation of moral life. Shaftesbury exercised an immense influence on succeeding generations and the whole of the Enlightenment and the Romantic movement evolved in the process of coming to terms with his philosophy. His enthusiasm found poetic utterance in his *Hymn to Nature* of 1709: 'O glorious Nature! supremely fair and sovereignly good! all-loving and all-lovely, all-divine!'

A concept of such breadth was not to be limited to trees and shrubs; nature is something much more in Shaftesbury's scheme of things – it is the universal working of forces which proceed from God and which all flow back towards a divine summation. Nature becomes the embodiment of unsullied creation, of all that is genuine and true; 'natural' things are things that develop without constraint, and this includes human thoughts and acts.

There can be no clearer 'natural' manifestation of this philosophy than the English style of landscape gardening of William Kent (1684–1748). Parks were designed by Kent as pieces of nature itself, in complete contrast to the

45

formal French park. In France parks and gardens expressed man's ability to compel nature to take on the forms of art; beauty was created at the dictates of human reason, triumphing over physical chaos. The English park, on the other hand, exemplified, not triumph, but surrender; emotion, not reason, prevailed. Walking through a landscaped garden aroused moods, and these in turn stimulated the depiction of landscape in art.

This outlook owed a considerable debt to England's island position. It is not easy to define the relationship that unquestionably exists between the emotional response to nature and the restlessness of a maritime people, between the interested observation of atmospheric phenomena and the love of the land that results from living in the country. The historical development was very closely allied to the feeling of being independent of the continent. No artistic canon restricted English painters, professional or dilettante, and among the benefits of this freedom must be included the liberty to cultivate an art form that was held in very low esteem in academic circles elsewhere in Europe.

In 1766 the German dramatist Gotthold Ephraim Lessing declared in his influential aesthetic treatise *Laokoon* that the only fit subject for the visual arts was the nude. He listed other possible subjects in descending order of merit, ending with landscape, 'for the beauty of landscape has nothing ideal about it'. The ensuing hundred years, the great age of academicism was dominated by the tragic and heroic emotions of Graeco-Roman art.

The difference between German and English aesthetic attitudes in the nineteenth century has been acutely summarized by Cornelius Gurlitt:

> While the Germans were debating the aesthetic and national value of buildings that were like so many Valhallas, an English artist was sitting by the wayside, painting the hazy sunlight, the dust, the gay throng of life. He saw beauty, not in the Platonic ideal, not in classic form, but in the chromatic impression of light and in atmospheric values. His name was Turner ...

Several circumstances allowed watercolour painting to flourish at that time in this one particular country: the cult of nature, with its strong emphasis on feeling and sentiment, an irrational religiosity, and the freedom in which personalities could develop. On these foundations, other factors were superimposed: a kind of nationalist ethos, looking for beauty in its own land; a yearning for the south, for the idealized beauty of the Campagna, as it appears in the work of Claude; the romantic notion of the Pathetic Fallacy, found in the work of Salvator Rosa. Finally, the silent contemplation of ruins aroused a historical instinct, an awed nostalgia for the past. Watercolour was the medium most capable of expressing these multiple stimuli and the confusing totality of inner tensions.

English landscapes of this period can be divided by their subjects into six groups. The aim of the 'ideal' landscape was not to reproduce a segment of reality, but to create instead an unreal perfection by imaginatively combining carefully selected elements, each beautiful in its own right. The scope of the 'romantic' landscape stretched from natural cataclysms to the sentimental view of history. The 'realistic' landscape was a relatively minor group, although realism was cogently represented in genre painting, which went far beyond its Dutch origins in the depiction and satirizing of manners. The nationalist ethos also gave rise to the 'indigenous' landscape as practised by the so-called 'Domestic Group' while the 'topographical' landscape was inspired by a more sober ambition: the faithful recording of festivals, events, towns and country houses, from palaces designed by Vanbrugh to more modest manors, with the owner and his household as accessory figures. The sixth group consists of all the scenes of travel, landscape, customs and adventures in foreign countries, ranging from personal reminiscences to scientific records; the desire to set down impressions of the world from Venice to South America presented watercolourists with some of their most rewarding subjects.

The great period of English watercolour painting, too little known outside England, divides chronologically into four generations of artists. The first, those born between 1700 and 1725 spanned the progression from monochromatic wash in bistre, indian and other inks, through the bichromaticism of brown foregrounds and pale blue backgrounds, already practised in Holland in the seventeenth century, to the use of a more subtly graded scale of tints; Alexander Cozens was one member of this generation. Differentiation of colour evolved in the work of the second generation, those born between 1725 and 1760, such as Gainsborough and J.R. Cozens. The third phase is dominated by Thomas Girtin and Turner, both born in 1775, who finally liberated watercolour painting from linear drawing. What may aptly be called a golden age was completed by a fourth generation, from the slightly younger contemporaries of Turner and Girtin down to Bonington.

The painter in the eighteenth century was beset by technical problems that have ceased to exist. He had to prepare and mix his own colours, relying on experiment and a store of tested recipes for his success. Papers were not made in adequate qualities for the most refined effects of watercolour; their absorbency was either too great or too little, and was in any case uneven in any one sheet of paper, so that the paint dried unevenly. When English papermakers eventually learned to manufacture a suitable paper, they stole a march of half a century on continental production and thus on the potential quality of continental watercolour painting.

The first really practical treatise on the materials and techniques of watercolour painting, the *Art of Drawing and Painting in Watercolour* appeared in

47

1770, and soon afterwards William Gilpin's poem *On landscape painting* was published, a work that ran into several editions, including foreign ones. Gilpin lays down six fundamental rules: (1) Enthusiasm for nature must be substantiated by careful study of its individual parts; (2) The parts should be judiciously selected to harmonize with the character of the whole; (3) Three planes, foreground, middle and background, are almost always more effective than more complicated arrangements and construction will be further improved if the scene centres on 'some principal commanding theme'; (4) Contrasts are essential but should be unforced; (5) All colours and densities can be achieved by thinning and mixing the three primary colours and the harmony of the whole stems from the light and shade so produced; (6) All figures should be appropriate to the landscape ('Say, does Abraham there / Ought that some idle peasant might not do?'). Gilpin closes with the recommendation that the finished work should be put on public exhibition, so that it may be judged impartially by men of taste.

Interesting light is thrown on the evolution of watercolour painting in England by a brief philological excursion into the origin of the word 'landscape'. It did not exist in 1606, the year in which Henry Peacham observed in his *Art of Drawing*: 'Landtskip is a dutch word.' A few years later Edward Norgate wrote in his *Miniatura*: 'Landscape, an art soe new in England, and so lately come ashore, as all the language within our fower seas cannot find it a name, but a borrowed one – the Dutch'. The term and the form alike came from the Dutch. The German word, *Landschaft*, also appears for the first time in a Dutch context, in Dürer's diary of his journey to the Netherlands in 1521. Two centuries later, it was the privilege of England to create, out of multifarious sources and circumstances, one of the loveliest phases in the whole history of art.

V THOMAS GIRTIN (London 1775–1802).
Rainbow over the Exe. Watercolour. 292:495 mm. Henry E. Huntington Library and Art Gallery, San Marino, Calif.
Like Turner, Girtin dispensed with the neutral underpainting, and laid his colour directly on to the paper with a full brush, in soft, ethereal shades.

VI JOHN CONSTABLE (East Bergholt, Suffolk 1776–1837 London).
Sky Study with Tree. Watercolour. 169:254 mm. British Museum, London.
The application of the paint in a system of blotches is typical of Constable and far in advance of the methods of his contemporaries.

V

VI

VII

VIII

The English Watercolourists

At the critical moment when a characteristically English painting emerged William Hogarth (1697–1764) was a key figure. It was in the academy which he opened in 1734 that an English style, resembling that of his engravings, evolved.

The tradition of the portrait miniature in England had begun with Hans Holbein the Younger (1497–1543). It was developed by Nicholas Hilliard (1547?–1619) and new ground was broken by the French Huguenot refugee, Isaac Oliver (died 1617), and his son Peter (died 1647). One of the greatest miniaturists was Samuel Cooper (1609–72). Edward Norgate's *Miniatura or the Art of Limning* (c. 1620, revised c. 1650) and his treatise *The Manner and Use of the Colours both for Picture by the Life, Landskip, History* became the standard texts on miniature painting and as such had great influence. The portrait miniature reached its greatest heights in the differing styles of John Smart (1741–1811) and Richard Cosway (1742–1821) on the one hand, and their younger contemporaries George Engleheart (1752–1829) and Andrew Plimer (1763–1837) on the other.

The painting of genre scenes of everyday life, derived from the realism of the Dutch School. A direct line of descent runs from Adriaen van Ostade to Isaac Cruikshank and Henry William Bunbury and from them, mingled now with the influence of Hogarth, to Thomas Rowlandson (1756–1827) and James Gillray (1757–1815), who found their true bent in the biting irony of their social and political satires.

It was during the eighteenth century that landscape assumed the position it has never again lost as the true subject of watercolour. Again, this can be traced to the influence of the numerous Dutch artists working in England in the seventeenth century, men like Cornelis van Poelenburg, Claude de Jongh, Hendrik van Steenwyk the younger and Alexander Keirincx. Their works were much in demand, since it was fashionable to have a picture of one's property painted in the Dutch manner, and a new generation grew up accustomed to seeing them in private collections, in town houses and in the country seats of the nobility.

The hunting scenes, country houses and landscapes of Peter Tillemans, who came to England from Flanders in 1708, set a pattern. English collectors, like English artists, were becoming better acquainted with the art of other countries; consequently they were in a position to recognize what things were typically English and naturally wanted to encourage the depiction of English scenes. Views of Dutch towns, like Ludolf Backhuysen's *Amsterdam* of 1702, were taken as the immediate model, but Italians like Marco Ricci and, a generation later, Francesco Zuccarelli, who arrived in England in the mid-century, not long after Canaletto, were equally influential.

Broadly speaking, there were two fundamentally different kinds of landscape, the idealized and the realistic – in the former, natural elements were arranged according to the promptings of the imagination to correspond to a subjective ideal; in the latter, an actual view was carefully copied with the aim of making a topographically exact record. The idealists claimed no less a figure than Claude as their patron. Turner bequeathed two of his paintings to the National Gallery on condition that they should be hung next to works by Claude, and his *Liber studiorum,* a compilation of engravings of landscape studies, was clearly modelled on the *Liber veritatis.* The different aims were reflected in differences of style. The visionary manner of painting in expansive, vehement patches and flecks of colour, with overpainting and merging of wet washes had an English precedent in the coloured costume designs of Inigo Jones (1573–1652) and was in direct contrast to the meticulous accuracy demanded in the reproduction of a view. The two extremes were pioneered by a well-matched pair: Alexander Cozens and Paul Sandby. A number of painters were already working in watercolour in the first half of the century, William Taverner and

VII JOSEPH MALLORD WILLIAM TURNER (London 1775–1851).
The Lake of Geneva and the Dent d'Oche from Lausanne. 1841. Watercolour. 227:330 mm.
British Museum, London.
All optical outlines are dissolved in a visionary impression of chromatic emotion.

VIII RICHARD PARKES BONINGTON (Arnold, Nottinghamshire 1801–28 London).
Off the English Coast. 1825. Watercolour. 141:231. Museum of Fine Arts, Budapest. Inv.
1935–2627.
A great and classic illustration of watercolour's power.

Samuel Scott for instance, but the most notable of them was the landscape painter Richard Wilson, who became the founder of the Italian Group after his journey to Italy in 1749, which brought him into contact with Zuccarelli and proved a turning point in his career. The year 1746 proved decisive in the development of watercolour painting in England, for it was in that year that Canaletto arrived in the country to begin a series of topographical *vedute* of English subjects, Richard Wilson presented two landscapes to the new Foundling Hospital in London, which aroused public interest in his realistic treatment of English scenery and Alexander Cozens went to Italy and began to paint his romantic visions of nature. These events had a decisive effect on the course of future developments.

Alexander Cozens was an experimenter and innovator. The sketchbook he brought back with him from Italy served as inspiration for the rest of his life. This is a point of some importance for, while his landscapes are very largely fanciful in character, a significant proportion of them are based on reality and the boundaries between the two worlds, visible and imaginary, are fluid. The principle was no different from Turner's practice, half a century later, of using things seen as a basis for the atmosphere and drama that were the true subjects of his paintings. Turner's visions, however, are suffused with colour, while Cozen's are virtually colourless betraying their closeness to the drawings tinted with monochrome wash from which they are derived (*pl. 8*).

If Cozens's colouring was nothing out of the ordinary for his time, his brushwork was an innovation of more than a technical kind. He expounded his aims in the *Essay to Facilitate the Invention of Landskips* and *A new Method of Assisting the Invention in Drawing Original Compositions of Landscape* (1784/85), but these drew scorn upon him from many quarters. According to an observer his method was 'to dash out, upon several pieces of paper, a number of accidentally large blots and loose flourishes, from which he selected forms and sometimes produced very grand ideas'.

Paul Sandby (1725–98) brought to landscape painting the meticulous precision that was necessary to his work as a draughtsman to the Ordnance Survey. He reached his peak around 1751 when he was living in Windsor with his brother Thomas, who was almost his equal as an artist. His best work presents the greatest possible contrast to that of Alexander Cozens, the colouring being pale and delicate, not particularly rich, but subtle. Unlike Cozens, Sandby was not a technical innovator; in the manner of his age, he first drew a precise outline, then applied shading with a neutral wash and only finally applied the colours.

Sandby's style found many successful imitators. Michael Angelo Rooker (1743–1801) painted scenes of country life in East Anglia and other parts of England and Wales with an evident love of his subjects. He represents an idealized view of the farmer's life held by many of his contemporaries. Rooker's paintings, and even more so those of Francis Towne (*c*. 1740–1816), occasionally display a toning-down of colour which almost reverts to monochrome though this tendency is no longer a result of naive simplicity, but rather a very controlled and conscious exploitation of muted tonal values. Among the followers of the Sandby brothers who are known as the 'Domestic' group, Thomas Hearne (1744–1817) occupies a special position. His chief works were published in 1807 in two volumes of engravings, dated 1779 to 1806, under the title *Antiquities of Great Britain*. The historical importance of the advances made by Sandby and the other topographers in depicting the English landscape cannot be rated too highly.

The Englishman who had made the Grand Tour began to exercise a considerable influence on artistic fashions and on the development of watercolour painting. Since the 'discovery' of Switzerland on the route to Italy he demanded views of Lake Geneva as well as atmospheric evocations of the Grand Canal, and the watercolourist was able to minister to his needs. Cause and effect were soon transposed: paintings of foreign scenes stimulated even more people to travel. The time became ripe for a reaction away from the topographical *veduta* towards re-creating the impression that a landscape made on the spirit and the emotions. This new attitude was reflected in the work of Thomas Gainsborough (1727–88). Although as a portrait painter he was the leading rival of Sir Joshua Reynolds, he saw in landscape a potential for emotional expressiveness that far surpassed its function as mere background in Reynold's work. He was not interested in the reproduction of specific views but was fascinated by nature as such and his depiction of landscape is relaxed, free and entirely subjective. Reynolds, on the other hand, was the supreme representative of academic rationalism; he became the president of the Royal Academy on its founding in 1768, and the coming conflict between watercolourists and academicians was already plainly adumbrated in the rivalry between the two great masters. Gainsborough's free, sketchy style, which grew out of a rejection of Dutch realism and was notably influenced by the landscapes of Van Dyck, was soon extremely popular.

The position thus gained was consolidated by the following generation of painters. From 1760 onwards watercolours were to be seen in the exhibitions of the Society of Artists of Great Britain and the medium grew in esteem until it was ranked equal to the 'great' art of oil-painting. The outstanding figure of this generation was John Robert Cozens (1752–97), the son of Alexander Cozens. In 1776, the year of his first visit to Italy, he exhibited at the Royal Academy; Turner said of this painting, *A Landscape, with Hannibal, in his March over the Alps, showing his Army the Fertile Plains of Italy*, that he had learned more from it than from any other picture. Cozens went to Italy again in 1782, with the eccentric writer William Beckford, and found the greatest inspiration of his life in the mountains of the Tyrol. Recognizing the purely painterly tensions between solid masses and the enveloping light, he rendered them in his watercolour drawings of Alpine scenes with a totally new method of colouring, floating the colours on to the paper with delicate variations of tonal strength. About ten years after his return to England, however, he succumbed to a 'total deprivation of the nervous faculty' and Dr Thomas Monro, the physician and patron who attended him until his death in 1797, became the key figure in the next stage of the development of watercolour painting.

At this time watercolour enjoyed an extraordinary popularity with amateurs, connoisseurs and private collectors, who bought and commissioned works, formed societies and opened their collections to the public. Dr Richard Mead was one of the first to do so, in 1754, and his example was followed shortly by the Duke of Richmond and soon by all the great collectors. Dr Thomas Monro (1759–1833), the son of a noted physician who was also a keen collector and connoisseur, not only adopted his father's profession but also surpassed him as a patron. Besides old masters, his collection included the early English watercolourists, Wilson, Sandby and Alexander Cozens, and Monro himself was a gifted amateur painter whose own watercolours bear comparison with those of his *protégés*. He attracted promising young artists to his house, fed them when it was hard for them to make ends meet, and paid them to copy works which he was unable to obtain in the original, which was good practice for them. The gathering of young men, 'rough diamonds', in his elegant household produced a cluster of talent that must have exceeded his wildest hopes. The 'Monro Boys' included J. R. Cozens, Thomas Girtin, J. M. W. Turner, John Sell Cotman, John Varley, Peter de Wint and Copley Fielding as well as a host of minor figures. Thomas Hearne assisted Monro in instructing his *protégés*, who began by copying items in Monro's collection and were later permitted to extend their capabilities by painting the views from the windows and terraces. Monro's influence lasted throughout his long life and made him one of the most remarkable figures in the history of English art at this period. Two of his pupils, Girtin and Turner rose to the greatest heights.

Thomas Girtin was born on 18 February 1775 and was orphaned at an early age. His talent became apparent while he was still very young and a painter called Fisher introduced him to Edward Dayes, a noted watercolourist. Pupil and teacher disagreed violently, however, so the Earl of Essex removed the boy to the studio of John Raphael Smith, where he was employed in colouring engravings. Then he met Turner. The friends started to look for subjects in nature and used to paint on the banks of the Thames. In 1788 they found employment colouring the drawings of an architect. They were eighteen years old when they first went to Dr Monro's house, where they copied everything available: Canaletto, Piranesi, George Morland, Thomas Hearne, Richard Wilson and above all John Robert Cozens. They divided the work: Girtin drew the outlines, Turner coloured them in, but soon, perhaps already while they were working together in this way, their paths began to diverge. Girtin toured England and Scotland in 1796. His works remain primarily topographical but his originality becomes increasingly obvious in his manner of applying brush to paper and the fluidity and transparency of his colour. He applied colour in large washes and added the small details afterwards, achieving extraordinary results from the very first. His treatment of his subjects is almost as faithful as in early *vedute* but no painter before him had ever been so successful in evoking the air, the faint smoke and haze of the atmosphere above views of towns and landscapes (*pls. V, 10*). Turner's approach to the world of appearances was quite different; only after an exhaustive study of all the possible methods employed by other artists, old and new, and preparing himself by long hours of copying and imitation, did he approach a subject, as though it was only thus that he found the desire to paint. Both artists, however, took a decisive and momentous step with their discovery of colour. They began to use local colour in shading, whether faint or heavy, instead of applying a grey underpainting, and thus their watercolours achieved a full and transparent

55

brilliance. Also, abandoning the practice of drawing outlines before starting to paint gave greater freedom in the application of the colour. In 1799 Girtin founded a drawing club, a forerunner of the Old Watercolour Society, which he did not live to see. This, however, fades into insignificance beside his technical achievement in accomplishing a fundamental change in the nature of watercolour, without which its potentialities could not have been fully realized. What had been prefigured in the work of J.R. Cozens was brought to fruition in the work of Girtin. De Wint, Varley, Bonington and others followed in his footsteps but he also opened the door to David Cox, John Sell Cotman and the genius of John Constable. In his lifetime Girtin remained relatively little known, but not long after his early death in 1802 he came to be recognized as the unsurpassable classic master of watercolour. Turner himself avowed: 'If Tom Girtin had lived I should have starved.'

Joseph Mallord William Turner was born on 23 April 1775 in Covent Garden in London, the son of a barber. He received his early training at the Royal Academy school, from 1789 to 1793, (this doubtless accounts for the strict academic outlook he retained all his life) and in the house of Dr Monro. He became an Associate of the Academy in 1799 and a full Academician in 1802. He travelled extensively, ceaselessly noting down his visual impressions, and mastered the depiction of the external world, both with topographic fidelity and, increasingly, in a freer manner as his brush technique became more relaxed and his colour increasingly transparent. This kind of mastery was not enough for him, however, and his urge to express subjective experiences became ever stronger. In 1807 Turner began to produce hasty sketches in which landscape is treated less and less as a compilation of given visible forms, and more and more as a context in which to display dramatic visual experiences. He became indifferent to the idea that a painting must appear finished in any conventional sense; unperturbed he went 'his solitary way into a new world of optical phenomena.' In his last works his painting of light reached the complete visionary resolution, which he had first begun to approach after his journey to Italy in 1819, so that light, colour and space melt and mingle in an indivisible whole, involving the spectator in an experience of nature that no longer proceeds from the surface of things but radiates from their innermost, fundamental reality (*pls. VII, 12*).

Throughout his life Turner was active and successful, travelling unceasingly in the Netherlands, the Rhine Valley, Switzerland, northern Italy and, above all, Venice. There could hardly be a stronger contrast than between his life and that of an artist who is his undoubted equal: John Constable. Constable (1776–1837) stands alone as a painter of nature and landscape and the occasional theatricality of Turner is quite absent from his work. Like Gainsborough, Constable confined his subjects to England. He travelled very little, devoting himself to one end – the truthful reproduction of nature and in the process discovering colours in an abundance that no one had ever before suspected. The climax of his career was the huge and unexpected success of his landscapes at the Paris Salon of 1824; they had a considerable influence on the rising generation of French artists, including Delacroix, Théodore Rousseau and most of the landscape painters of the mid-nineteenth century (*pl. VI*).

Beside the pre-eminent figure of Constable, a number of other artists stand out among the multitude who helped to bring the watercolour landscape to its fullest maturity in the first half of the new century in England. One of the most important was John Sell Cotman (1782–1842), a member of the Norwich School founded by John Crome. Like so many young artists he worked for a time copying and colouring under the aegis of Dr Monro, but he soon developed an outstandingly free style, characterized by a sublime simplicity, achieved by flat washes of colour in calm, cool shades. He received no recognition during his lifetime. His best works were all painted fairly early in his life, during his travels about England and Wales between 1803 and 1805 (*pl. 9*).

Girtin's influence is most evident in the work of John Varley (1778–1842) and Peter de Wint (1784–

IX HEINRICH FRIEDRICH FÜGER (Heilbronn 1751–1818 Vienna).
Queen Caroline of Naples. 1790. Watercolour and opaque white on ivory. 176:128 mm. (oval). Albertina, Vienna. Inv. 30,194.
Queen Caroline, a daughter of Empress Maria Theresa, was the artist's patron from the time when he was studying in Italy. The portrait illustrates all the typical characteristics of Füger's technique: dots and very freely drawn strokes of colour are applied with the point of a full brush, bringing the painted surface vividly to life.

IX

X

1849). They captured the true face of the English scene, the atmosphere and character of towns and villages, in a highly polished, painterly manner, avoiding both idealization of a honeyed pastoral existence and romantic overemphasis on the wildness of untamed nature.

In spite of his early death, Richard Parkes Bonington (1801–28) was a major figure of this period in every field of painting, though his influence was even stronger in France than in England. As a boy he was a pupil of François Louis Francia, the friend of Girtin, in Calais, and later worked in Paris where he became a friend of Delacroix. The radiant brilliance of his highlights was much admired, by Corot among others, and indeed the luminosity of his paintings has never really been equalled. Many of the advances made by succeeding generations of French painters would not have been possible if Bonington had not cleared the way by the freedom of his brushwork and his escape from the restraint of rigid outlines. His influence, indirect in the work of Eugène Isabey, endured long enough to have had a direct effect on Eugène Boudin and Claude Monet (*pl. VIII*).

In connection with the development of watercolour painting in England, a few words must be said about the various societies that were formed, since so much of what we admire of the watercolourists' work can only be explained in the light of their concerted aims and efforts. By the early nineteenth century the Royal Academy was well established and respected, including Turner and Constable, who became an Academician in 1829, among its members. In the course of time, however, its annual exhibitions had become less and less suitable as a context for showing watercolours, and watercolourists eventually decided to form an independent institution. The exclusive and influential Society of Painters in Watercolours was founded in 1804 and its first members included Joshua Cristall, Sawrey Gilpin, Nicholas Pocock and John Varley. Regular exhibitions were held with the intention of raising watercolour to the status enjoyed by the classic media. The Society's prime object was to defend the absolute purity of watercolour against contamination with body colour or any other admixture and pure watercolour soon came to be looked on as a peculiarly English medium. The Society was indeed so exclusive that in 1807 another was founded, the Associated Artists in Watercolour, which survived only a few years. It was followed by a New Society (whereupon the original society came to be known as the Old Watercolour Society) whose members included all the great artists of this period, when watercolour painting was at its zenith, and its exhibitions were events of national importance. Its subsequent decline was as rapid as that of the English watercolour itself; this is not to say that great heights have not been reached since, by Frank Brangwyn and Russell Flint in recent years, and by William Callow, John Glover and others in the past, but the original exclusivity of the society was lost in its subsequent development.

The last member of the English school of watercolourists who must be mentioned is the American James Abbott McNeill Whistler (1834–1903). Born the son of an engineer in Lowell, Massachusetts, he was brought up in Russia and went to West Point Military Academy, but in 1855 he decided to study art in Paris. He worked mainly in England, where he was very successful, becoming a member of the Society of British Artists in 1884 and its president in 1887, but he continued to spend a good deal of time in Paris. The change in the general attitude to nature is illustrated by the connections that Whistler himself made between his paintings and music, often giving them titles such as *Nocturne* or *Harmony*. He said, in the famous *Ten O'Clock Lecture* in 1885:

> Nature contains the elements, in colour and form, of all pictures as the keyboard contains the notes of all music. But the artist is born to pick and choose, and group with science those elements, that the result may be beautiful – as the musician gathers his notes and forms his chords, until he brings forth from chaos glorious harmony.

The influence of the art of the Far East on Whistler is well known and it may well be that the allusive, elliptical style of his watercolours owes something to it. In these works Whistler takes English watercolour painting to its furthest conclusions and beyond, to the threshold of a new era.

X RUDOLF VON ALT (Vienna 1812–1905).
The Anio Gorge near Tivoli. 1835. Watercolour. 333:260 mm. Albertina, Vienna. Inv. 32,571.
This view shows how the twenty-three-year-old artist has evolved a new way of indicating the presence of a secondary source of light in the illumination of outlines. In 1835 Alt visited Rome, Naples and Capri and the journey marked the beginning of a great career.

From Classicism to Realism: Germany, Switzerland and Austria in the Eighteenth and Nineteenth Centuries

From the Renaissance onwards, humanists had seen it as their prime duty to widen the knowledge of the world and of man. The perception of this duty was still new when Pico della Mirandola (1463–1494) declared: 'God made man on the last day of creation, so that he should recognize the laws of the universe, love its beauty and admire its grandeur.' Recognition, love and admiration were the paths by which generations of German artists strove to grasp reality. Maria Sibylla Merian (1647–1717), who was brought up in this tradition of the late Renaissance and whose own meticulous paintings of flowers and animals in watercolour and body colour display a mastery of both media, made a typical comment on the transformation of caterpillars into butterflies, a process which she had observed and recorded in her pictures: 'As often as it happened, [we] praised and glorified God's peculiar omnipotence and wonderful regard for such insignificant creatures and lowly birds.' In the introduction to her three-volume study of caterpillars, *Das Raupenbuch* (the full title runs 'The miraculous transformation of caterpillars and their curious diet of flowers'), she defined the purpose of her studies as 'to increase God's glory by means of his creatures'.

Baroque artists had a number of uses for watercolour: in studies from nature, backgrounds, still-lifes, coloured designs and sketches for oil-paintings, murals or ceiling paintings. From the sixteenth to the eighteenth century it was most regularly used, particularly in Germany, in a rather mediocre art form, the decoration of albums. These albums contain many examples of a conscious revival of traditional landscape painting in the manner of Dürer for, from the Reformation onwards, watercolour had been the usual medium for depicting scenes from the lives of ordinary people. They are unquestionably of value to the social historian first and foremost, 'a kind of protest of the middle classes against painting which did not pay enough attention to their needs' (Brieger), but in some pages it is possible to discern the first signs of a developing interest in nature. Album decoration reached its height in the eighteenth century, and preserves much of the charm and brilliance of that delightful era, but as long as no really outstanding works had been executed in watercolour it remained a minor art. Even though the German Daniel Nicholas Chodowiecki (1726–1801), for instance, sometimes used watercolour, his best works were drawings in sinopia or indian ink.

Then, in the early eighteenth century, watercolour acquired a more important function as the copyist's medium. The growth in demand for copies of great works sprang from a variety of motives. Idealists in the age of the Enlightenment hoped that the propagation of beauty would lead to a moral elevation of humanity. The advantages to the copyist of the smaller formats and the simpler techniques of watercolour painting, had already come to be recognized during the late baroque and rococo era and smaller paintings now seemed better suited to the more modest life of a growing bourgeoisie. Thus the rise of watercolour beyond its original ancillary status was closely bound up with the rise of the middle classes.

The initial impetus for the recognition of watercolour as an independent artistic medium in Germany did not come from France, which led the way in so many aspects of manners and art in the eighteenth century, but from Holland. It is also true, however, that Dutch influence did often reach Germany by way of France: Georg Wille, for example, a German who worked in Paris, had numerous pupils who returned to Germany and spread his '*holländernde Manier*', a significant new attitude to landscape. In his life of Hackert Goethe writes:

> In August 1765 Philipp Hackert and young Dunker arrived in Paris. The well-known engraver Wille took them out into the country to draw with him, but Philipp Hackert found small joy in the fiddling task of cramming the miserable little hovels of peasants, with their cabbage patches and stunted fruit trees, on to a quarto sheet, for his eye and hand were used to great subjects ...

But seventeenth-century Dutch artists such as Herman van Swanenveld, Nicolaes Berchem and Cornelis van Poelenburg also exercised a strong direct influence on young German landscapists, if only through the galleries, collections and museums which were suddenly opening everywhere.

In 1762 Christian Ludwig Hagedorn, who became director general of the Saxon Academy of Art in Dresden in the following year, published his *Betrachtungen über die Malerei* ('Observations on Painting'), a work which provides evidence of the leading cultural role played by Saxony under Augustus the Strong. Hagedorn's statement that 'The taste for what is morally beautiful and the taste for the arts flow from one and the same source' came to be regarded almost as a religious truth. For a time all developments were dominated by this classic equation of beauty and goodness which closely corresponded to what Johann Joachim Winckelmann, in his *Gedanken über die Nachahmung der griechischen Werke* ('Thoughts on the Imitation of Greek Works') (1755), had expounded to a generation of young Germans hoping for a new dawn: art as an expression of 'noble simplicity and tranquil greatness', instead of the 'impudent fire' of the baroque. We know the impression that the artist Adam Friedrich Oeser made on Goethe when he taught him this principle in 1770: 'it will have consequences throughout my whole life'. But while Winckelmann aimed at the ideal, at the 'idea' given form as transcendent reality, watercolours, even those painted by Oeser, are a total denial of the concept. Since the most suitable form for the representation of the ideal was the most abstract, line became the principal medium of classicism and watercolour, because of its essentially painterly, anti-linear qualities, was thought to have an air of 'untruthfulness'. Winckelmann and Oeser both started from the conviction that the 'idea', in the Platonic sense, must have already manifested itself in antiquity in the most elevated form possible. Their conclusion was completely logical: the modern artist could approach the 'ideal' only by imitating the art of antiquity as faithfully as possible. This principle was adopted by the academies who took it to absurd extremes: since the great masters of painting had already created sublime works, the only task of the pupil who wished to reach the same heights was to copy those works. Such reasoning inevitably led to the absurd conclusion that if the senses are only capable of perceiving the raw material, while the human spirit has elevated the material through art, the copy of a work of art is superior to the original, because it has been refined in the spirit not once but twice. It is, however, quite clear that Winckelmann never meant the simple copying of works when he spoke of imitation, although his thesis is still sometimes misunderstood. At its heart lie the concepts of *mimesis* and *ethos*. By *mimesis* Winckelmann meant that the 'idea' inhabiting an object was what should be imitated, that the reproduction of an object's form should reveal its *ethos* and he was thus concerned with spiritual rather than physical form. Nevertheless, belief in the disparity between nature and art was so deeply rooted that at the beginning of the nineteenth century Hegel was still able to say, in his *Ästhetik*:

> It might well be asserted that beauty in art is superior to nature. For beauty in art is beauty born and reborn out of the spirit, and inasmuch as the spirit and its products are superior to nature and its appearances, so beauty in art is superior to the beauty of nature.

Germany and Switzerland

Throughout the whole of this period, creative energies were divided between two divergent currents, the one anti-naturalistic and linear, the other naturalistic and painterly. In this book we are only concerned with the latter, with those artists who expressed form in terms of colour, light and shade and for whom true watercolour, as opposed to coloured, but essentially linear, drawing, was a sympathetic medium. The classic school is largely irrelevant in this context, therefore, but one member should at least be mentioned: Jacob Philipp Hackert (1737–1807), one of the leading German artists of his generation. Born in Prenzlau in Brandenburg, he studied in Berlin where, at the instigation of Le Sueur, the director of the Academy, he made his first essays in landscape, copying Claude and the Dutch School. He went on to paint the first large landscapes from nature, but his contacts with painting in France in the mid-1760s led him to a freer depiction of nature from his imagination. The acclaim his work received in Rome and Naples and his travels in the Campagna and Sicily made him a leading figure of his generation. Significantly, his closest contacts in Rome, were with English artists like Richard Payne Knight, whom he and J. R. Cozens accompanied to Sicily in 1776–9.

Josef Anton Koch (1768–1839) was perhaps the most violent opponent the academies ever had. He went to the Charles Academy in Stuttgart in 1785, but left it because the teaching of art there 'wavered between a shallow and enfeebled Baroque and an even more uncertain Classicism', and went to Strasbourg. Koch was the son of a Tyrolese farmer and his emotional response to the grandeur of nature was unusually powerful. His travels in Switzerland from 1792 to 1794 made an impression on him that lasted for the rest of his life. He rejected straightforward imitation of nature as something unworthy of the name of art, but he was a landscape painter before all else and his watercolours are the first of his generation that stand comparison with work of the very highest order.

Not surprisingly Swiss artists soon began to paint mountain scenery. On the advice of his teacher, Heinrich Wuest (1741–1821) went to Amsterdam in 1760 and then to Paris in 1766. Returning to Zurich in 1769, he opened a studio which became the centre of the new movement. Caspar Wolf (1735–98) was one of the first to take the mountains of his homeland for his subject. Between 1775 and 1777 he painted a series of Swiss views in watercolour and his major

work, *Alpes Helveticae*, became very well known. The highly imaginative and romantic style, in which he depicts foaming avalanches and glaciers dissolving into frothy *rocaille*, evidently owes much to the influence of *Die Alpen*, a poem published in 1729 by Albrecht von Haller, the Swiss philosopher of the early Enlightenment, which laid the foundations for the belief in the healing purity of nature.

This sentimental idealization eventually led to Rousseau's exhortations to a return to nature, which determined the whole romantic character of the age. Goethe, who found the mountains 'terrible', none the less prized the work of Johann Ludwig Aberli (1723–86), seeing in him the real founder of the Swiss school of *vedutisti*. Like every other artist of his generation, Aberli began by copying other people's works, but on learning from Sandrart's biography of Claude, that even this paragon, held up to every beginner as a model, had painted directly from nature, he decided to do the same. Other Swiss *vedutisti* followed: Peter Birrmann, Johann Jacob Biedermann and Ludwig Hess (1760–1800). In his short life Hess painted some delicate, airy watercolours, which are of real merit. The Swiss tradition of mountain landscape culminated in the great gouaches of Alexandre Calame (1810–64), a native of Geneva and the most famous of all the nineteenth-century painters of Alpine scenery.

The cultural atmosphere in Germany was ideal for the rise of watercolour. A movement started in Dresden, led by Alexander Thiele (1685–1752), who deserves credit as the first German painter of landscapes in watercolour. Early in his career he painted in body colour but the tendency in his later work, even more pronounced in the work of Christoph Nathe (1753–1806), who was perhaps his superior, is to thin the paint to the point of transparency and to leave the white paper blank as an element of the composition. A painter of the highest promise was lost with the early death of Johann Georg Wagner (1744–67), who experimented with mixing watercolour and gouache, a technique which only came into its own much later.

By the end of the century the most important developments in watercolour were taking place in Munich. The general movement did not really take hold there until quite late, the decisive event being the arrival of the Kobell family from Mannheim in 1793. Ferdinand Kobell's work in Mannheim was very much in the Dutch tradition and is surpassed by that of his son, Wilhelm Kobell (1766–1855), the founder of a distinct Munich School, which included Max Josef Wagenbauer and Georg Dillis. Although

63

Wilhelm Kobell's early works are also in the 'holländernde Manier', they already show a great degree of freedom and he soon learned to make the best artistic use of the transparency of his colours.

But while German artists made technical advances independently, it was to Italy, rather than to their own homeland, that the young German romantics turned for subject matter and inspiration. In his essay on landscape painting (1803–06), Carl Ludwig Fernow declares: 'No, my friend! Not here, but there is the proper climate of art! The German artist must live, strive and create in Italy.' Italy was the crucial formative experience of the whole generation and thither the young romantics went in search of the Middle Ages and the beauty of the Campagna. Inspired by the south, Heinrich Nathe evolved schemes of pale greys, greens and blues, with subtle and sensitive distinctions of colouring that were almost without precedent in German art and remained unequalled until the advent of the impressionists. The outstanding achievement in this generation, however, was that of Johann Christian Reinhart (1761–1847), who eventually settled in Rome. Although his early inclinations and training would seem to have destined him to be a realist, Reinhart overthrew academic pedantry completely and ended as an idyllist. Ludwig Richter (1803–84), who admired him greatly, wrote in Rome:

> ... the dust filling the academies and museums, the lumber of faded rules and maxims that I was exposed to from my infancy and had painfully tried to observe – these were swept away and thrown overboard here. Back in Germany, art was freezing to death under a cold blanket of winter ...

Romantic opposition to the academies was founded on three principal arguments: adherence to strict rules contradicted the freedom of genius; the composition of a work of art by selecting isolated elements was a denial of the truth that the whole ought to express; copying the works of accepted masters did not lead to the discovery of the Platonic Idea, but only hindered the development of individual, personal styles. The most extreme rejection came from the group of young romantics in Rome known as the Nazarenes, who found their ideal in the Middle Ages and strove to emulate the purity of the gothic masters. The strong element of nationalism in this movement was certainly connected with the initial revulsion against the terror that accompanied the revolution in France and the subsequent struggle against the dominion of Napoleon. The stark realities of the Napoleonic wars naturally made a strong impression on other artists, including watercolourists,

and the inevitable consequence was a long overdue turn towards realism. Johann Adam Klein (1792–1875) recorded troops on the move, their waggons and horses, the figures of people he met on the road on his extensive travels, in fresh and vivid watercolours. The Congress of Vienna of 1814–15 sought to restore the *status quo*, but it could not stem the new currents in art and the young generation that turned once more to Italy was one on which realism had left an ineradicable stamp. The new realism found a particularly strong foothold in Düsseldorf, where an especial interest was taken in genre painting in watercolour; the best work of this kind was done by Oswald and Andreas Achenbach.

Romanticism, however, followed a rather different course. The earliest romantic artists had preferred to work with line, but this was no longer true of Caspar David Friedrich (1774–1840). No one else has ever been so strongly moved by the inner vision which compels an artist to paint what he sees within him rather than before him. Armed with an unparalleled instinct for colour, Friedrich went directly to nature itself. By this means he achieved ends that others were only able to aim for – the sense of melting into space and distant prospects, the creation of an atmosphere in which melancholy is a living presence. Rarely has nature been endowed with such depths of soul as in the paintings of Friedrich. His experience of nature was all-embracing, all-loving and all-animating. It was complemented by the theories of Philipp Otto Runge (1777–1810), an important romantic artist who was deeply influenced by his contacts with Friedrich, at the academy in Dresden and by the writings of Ludwig Tieck and Friedrich Schlegel. Runge's chief conviction was that history painting had had its day; to achieve new heights the art of the future would have to follow a mystical symbolism best expressed through landscape.

In the ferment of the decades at the beginning of the nineteenth century, Munich continued to play a leading role. Besides the Kobell family and their many followers, Karl Rottmann (1797–1850) is a figure of some importance. In certain respects he was inclined to classicism and followed Koch, but his decisive characteristic is the combination of a kind of heroic romanticism with a new topographical realism in landscape painting. He painted several series of historical landscapes for King Ludwig I of Bavaria and the watercolour studies and sketches for these, together with the studies he made while travelling in Italy and Greece, constitute one of the finest achievements in German watercolour painting (*pl. 19*).

A very similar synthesis is evident in the work of Ernst Fries (1801–33). After receiving a conventional education, Fries made his way, via Karlsruhe and Munich, to Rome, where Ludwig Richter hailed him as 'highly talented' (*pl. 20*). He quickly gained recognition on his return to Germany but died regrettably young.

The goal at which artists now aimed was absolute fidelity, uniting the painterly values of volume and light with linear exactitude, and recreating the grace of the subject with loving intuition. A study in the Kupferstichkabinett in Dresden, *Alpine Valley* by Karl Philipp Fohr (1795–1818), is typical: the colour is only partially laid on, in delicate primary shades, unbroken and insubstantial.

The centre of artistic influence now moved to Berlin. The Berlin school of watercolour painting grew out of the depiction, not of landscape, but of architecture, and was motivated less by a response to nature than by the search for reality. The earliest views are naive in the extreme: all that need be said of them is that they prepared the ground for the middle-class, urban genre paintings of Carl Graeb and Adolph Schrödter. They were surpassed, in this field, however, by Theodor Hosemann (1807–75), whose delicate, ethereal studies are relaxed and free, hardly inferior to those of Franz Krüger (1797–1857), whose watercolour portraits enjoyed a much greater success. The outstanding personality of the Berlin school, however, was Carl Blechen (1798–1840), who overshadowed even Karl Rottmann, his senior by only a few months. He too began with architectural views, but the studies from his Baltic trip of 1828 are already strikingly original, unprecedented at that date in their impressionistic approach. He wields his implements, brush and pen, with a relaxed hand, his visual grasp of the subject is rapid and realistic, but his composition is always perfectly balanced. His journey to Italy of 1828–29 produced the sketchbooks and views of Naples, Capri and Salerno, some of which are among the finest work of the period. Blechen had studied under Caspar David Friedrich in Dresden, but this was evidently of less importance in his development than his encounter with Turner in Italy. From that moment on Blechen was intoxicated with the play of line and colour, which became the one, all-important subject of his work (*pl. 23*).

Berlin produced one more artist of even greater stature, Adolf Menzel (1815–1905), in whom this period of German watercolour found its ultimate fulfilment. He was extremely versatile, working in oil, pastels and pure body colour, and above all, in a medium he invented for himself, a mixture of watercolour and gouache, which gives his work a totally individual stylistic character. With the exception of a few sketches, Menzel never painted in pure watercolour but pursued the use of his hybrid '*Aquarellgouache*' until he was a very old man and with it reached the furthest limits of artistic expression and formal virtuosity. On his first visit to Paris in 1855, Menzel found that a similar mixed medium had just been adopted by the *chroniqueurs*, but it seems certain that he had already evolved his own version of it before the contact with Meissonier.

Austria

During the century or so that elapsed between the aristocratic glitter of the late Rococo and the sentimental historicism of the late nineteenth century, the pulse of art in Vienna beat to the same rhythms as in the rest of the German-speaking world. There were, however, certain fundamental differences. In the eighteenth century, as Goethe recorded, Vienna still enjoyed a special regard in the eyes of every German as the capital of the Holy Roman Empire; during the Napoleonic wars it was the rallying point of romantic hopes for national victory over the French; and lastly, in the nineteenth century, it became a centre of economic and social expansion. These three phases were reflected in the art of the time. From the middle of the eighteenth century increasing numbers of German artists flocked to Vienna, bringing with them a variety of outlooks, theories and principles. They included some of the great names in the history of German art: Brand, Füger, Alt, Rahl, Gauermann, Runk, Klein, Erhard, Olivier, Schnorr, Heinrich, Overbeck, Pforr, Agricola and Krafft.

The early works of Johann Christian Brand (1722–95) are charming landscapes completely within the Rococo tradition. However he soon broke free from this mould to pursue nature at first hand and his studies are among the finest examples of watercolour painting in Austria. He found an audience for his views at the academy in Vienna, founded as early as 1692 and given a new lease of life after 1766 under Jakob Schmutzer (1733–1811). Schmutzer, who had studied under J. G. Wille in Paris, established a new approach to reality; he advocated 'the study of nature in broad daylight'. This was something quite unheard of, as was proved by the adventure of a class from the academy which was taken by the gifted Franz Edmund Weirotter to study the waterfalls at Gaming – it narrowly escaped arrest for espionage!

The Vienna Academy played an important role in the development of the medium. One of its directors, Heinrich Friedrich Füger (1751–1818), became the acknowledged master of the classic portrait miniature painted in watercolour on ivory (*pl. IX*). He used body colour very rarely and then only for highlighting; normally he wielded a full brush with incredible freedom on the small piece of ivory. He used pale reds for the underpainting and, by shading with layers of transparent colour, gave faces an unusual vitality and attractiveness.

Austrian watercolour painting of this period falls into two main groups: studies of human subjects, in portraiture and genre, and aspects of nature, in *vedute* and landscapes. Carl Schütz (1745–1800), was a pioneer in the field of town views, especially of Vienna. He formed a partnership with Johann Ziegler (c. 1750–c. 1812) in 1778, and not long afterwards they were joined by the landscape artist Laurenz Janscha (1749–1812). The fifty-seven studies, out of a projected series of eighty, that the trio produced by 1798 became very well known in numerous editions and reproductions, and created a demand for more of the same kind of thing.

Young watercolourists continued to come to Vienna from all over Germany and Austria. On 21 April 1801 the academy granted leave to 'Ferdinand Runk, born in Freiburg, landscape painter, to copy landscape subjects in the Tyrol'. The studies Runk painted, armed with this permit, gave Archduke Johann of Austria the idea of commissioning a series of watercolour views of all the finest scenes in his Alpine estates, a project which occupied a number of artists for several decades. One was Jakob Gauermann (1773–1843), who was set up for life by the commission to paint a complete topography of the duchy of Styria in watercolour; another was Matthäus Loder (1781–1828), a sensitive and attractive personality in whose work realism, genre and Romantic enthusiasm mingle with persuasive charm. When Loder died of a pulmonary disease in 1828, the archduke entrusted the continuation of the series to Thomas Ender (1793–1875), a watercolourist who had already enjoyed considerable success. While still

a student at the academy, impervious to the influences of heroic and idealized landscape painting, Ender found his subject-matter in countryside around Vienna and recorded it in a simple, uncontrived manner, avoiding self-conscious ancillary motifs and figures. In 1817 he was chosen by the Chancellor, Prince Metternich, to accompany the Austrian expedition to Brazil, from which he returned exhausted but with no less than 782 studies in his portfolio. These met with the approval of the academy and were instrumental in popularizing a free and relaxed technique. Meanwhile the emperor recalled to Vienna another artist, Joseph Rebell (1787–1828), who had chosen an independent existence in Italy in preference to the academic rigidity of Vienna. Many younger artists were influenced by his work, particularly by his use of the effects of two opposing sources of light.

The Biedermeier period produced a number of watercolour painters, but only one miniaturist who could rival the excellence of Füger. Moritz Michael Daffinger (1790–1849) was in fact one of Füger's pupils, but was also strongly influenced by Sir Thomas Lawrence, who spent some time in Vienna in 1819. Daffinger became the 'Austrian Isabey', but in his later work turned to flower painting, in which he achieved an unrivalled perfection. Another exponent of the Viennese style of portraiture was Johann Grund (1808–87), who studied in Vienna, his home town, but settled in Karlsruhe, after extensive travels (*pl. 17*). Josef Kriehuber (1800–76), an artist of virtually inexhaustible energy and stamina, painted 'all Austria' and thus left behind him an unusually comprehensive portrait of the human face in his age. Austrian watercolour painting, which became increasingly a Viennese preserve, reached another height in the work of Peter Fendi (1796–1842). His training as a copyist in the imperial numismatic collection taught him a miniaturist's regard for precision which he combined with a marvellously free brush technique. His transparent colour sheds a radiance over his affectionate genre depictions of groups and interiors, which became some of the most sought-after works of art in Vienna during the Biedermeier

XI Eugène Delacroix (Charenton Saint-Maurice 1798–1863 Paris).
Interior of a Moorish House. Watercolour over pencil, with notes in pencil. 160:215 mm. Louvre, Paris. Album R.F. 9. 154, fol. 38.
In January 1832, Delacroix went to Algeria, where his colouring underwent a decisive transformation. This unassuming little sketch plainly shows the new significance that light flooding into a space now had for him; it is the basic element in which all the colours are dynamically revealed.

XI

XII

period (*pl. 22*). A circle of talented young artists gathered round Fendi, Carl Schindler, Albert Schindler, Friedrich Treml, and the picture of manners, of which Josef Danhauser (1805–45) was the prime exponent, became one of the characteristic genres of Viennese Biedermeier; it comprised some of the outstanding work of the period and survived it, to be represented later in the century by, for instance, Johann and Ludwig Passini.

The changing artistic fashions of almost the whole of the nineteenth century are bridged by the work of a single man, whose *œuvre* constitutes Austria's major contribution to the history of watercolour: Rudolf von Alt (1812–1905) (*pls. X, 18*). His father, Jakob Alt (1789–1872), had left his native Frankfurt and settled in Vienna where he soon established a reputation as a watercolourist. He travelled extensively and even as a child Rudolf started to accompany him, at first as an assistant, but soon outstripping him in ability. Together they looked for subjects in a wide area of Austria, Italy and the Habsburg crown estates and painted a number of works commissioned by the court, including a series of 129 watercolour *vedute* in a large format, designed to amuse the feeble-minded Ferdinand I. Rudolf von Alt brought to the depiction of nature an intuition learned in the picture of manners, which raises his landscapes to a level far above the normal run of *vedute*. Throughout his life he remained an astonishingly independent figure, standing apart from all movements, obsessed by one purpose: to record the visual appearance, the beauty, colour and vitality of a sunlit world. He finally evolved a new, free and very personal technique, a kind of 'drawing in watercolour', which is fundamentally different from the technique of any other artist. His mode of composition was to paint isolated points of crystallization, leaving the rest of the paper blank, and juxtaposing dark and light colour contrasts without any intermediary shades. The resulting effect of spontaneity which makes his work so vivid unites a modern immediacy with genuine artistic tension. In the 1890s Alt was elected leader of the Vienna Secession, the Austrian *avant-garde*, and although by then in his eighties, he assured the astonished Franz Joseph I that he still felt young enough 'to start again and again at the beginning'.

Watercolour painting in Austria reached the apogee of technical virtuosity represented in France by Meissonier and in Germany by Menzel in the work of August von Pettenkofen (1822–89), a painter of peasant life, particularly in the Hungarian realm of the Dual Monarchy. Finally the old era came to an end in the work of Anton Romako (1832–89) whose tortured sensitivity prefigures the tensions expressed later in the following century by the expressionists and, in portraiture, by Oskar Kokoschka.

XII Gustave Moreau (Paris 1826–98).
Beside the Waters. Watercolour. 270:370 mm. Autograph title in the bottom right-hand corner: *Près des Eaux.* Musée National Gustave Moreau, Paris.
As always in Moreau's work, the recumbent female figure symbolizes a mysterious force. To the contrasts of heat and coolness in the colours, between the vitality in the texture of the paper (brought out by the use of an almost dry brush) and the languor of the figure, is added a tension between space and light that wraps the whole in mystery.

France in the Eighteenth and Nineteenth Centuries

French art in the eighteenth century was dominated by two main currents: rationalist academicism, the ossified inheritance of Poussin and Claude, and the graceful, often rather precious style known as the rococo. The strong call for a 'return to nature', raised by the anti-rationalist philosopher Jean-Jacques Rousseau, marked the appearance of a rather nostalgic form of realism, within rococo art, which foreshadows the romaticism and the realism of nineteenth-century French art.

The key figure in this development, as far as watercolour is concerned, is Jean-Honoré Fragonard (*pl. 13*). In his full-scale canvases he handles rather frivolous themes with enormous charm; his studies reveal, if anything, even greater virtuosity of brushwork and, although he never used pure watercolour, he achieved great variety in monochrome washes ranging from gallnut ink (originally black although oxydation has turned it brown in surviving works), through the greyish blacks of Chinese ink, to the beautiful shades of pale brown bistre (*pl. 13*). (The occasional application of the term sepia is usually incorrect since sepia, a reddish-brown pigment made from cuttlefish ink, was unknown before 1775.) The refinement of Fragonard's chiaroscuro, achieved with a loaded brush, is the height of virtuosity and his dynamism and intensity make him the forerunner of all Romantic art. When he was in Rome, in 1756, he became friendly with a pensioner at the Academy, Hubert Robert; together they attended classes, absorbed all the impressions of the Eternal City and paid their respects to the great masters. When it all proved too much for them, they took refuge in the countryside outside the city, finding a completely new world in the landscape. The result is shown in works like Fragonard's *Villa d'Este* in the Albertina, with its vibrant brushwork, and in Robert's numerous fresh, bright watercolours depicting the parks and ruins of Rome with delicate sentimentality. However, artists like Robert who used watercolour were a minority; in the eighteenth century the media most used throughout Europe were pen and ink, crayon, sinopia and, in particular, pastel, which enjoyed an especial popularity among artists from Rosalba Carriera to Jean-Étienne Liotard. The only form of water-soluble colour commonly used was gouache.

Even in the portrait miniature, which was as popular in France as in England in the eighteenth century, the medium most favoured was a mixture of opaque and transparent colours, which allowed very subtle effects in the representation of skin and clothing. French miniature painting, long dominated by Pierre Adolphe Hall (1739–83) reached a peak in the work of François Dumont (*pl. 16*), who was in turn surpassed by Jean-Baptiste Isabey (*pl. 14*). Isabey's exceptional facility made him an institution, outliving his original patrons at the court of Louis XVI and surviving through the vicissitudes of revolution, empire and restoration into the nineteenth century. It was said that he painted ladies 'as they hoped to look', though this is perhaps a rather sarcastic judgment.

The epitome of art under the empire was expressed in the great oil paintings of Roman and imperial themes by Jacques-Louis David (1748–1825). His manifesto of 1794 proclaims: 'To paint the energy of a people which has proclaimed the liberty of the human race, requires proud colours, a powerful brush and vulcanic genius.' The essential nature of watercolour was ill-suited to heroic painting of this order, which soon became the only style acknowledged by the academies, or to the classicism of Ingres whose fundamental emphasis on line and drawing embodied the academic ideal. It might therefore seem supremely logical that the movement against academicism, the protest against '*le style*', should have turned to watercolour, but there were of course more profound reasons for the development than sheer contrariness. It was characteristic of this Romantic counter-movement in every respect that line should be replaced in importance by unlimited planes, and the outline of form by imprecise blots, that the cool shades chosen to evoke marble antiquity should give way to the blaze of strong colouring, and that the remote classical subjects should be rejected in favour of themes from France's own history. Romanticism in France did not mean the misty German forests of Caspar David Friedrich; it meant the passion, violence, genius, spontaneity and strength of natural colour that we find in Géricault. The first duty of a picture, according to Delacroix, was to be a feast for the eyes.

The conflict between idealism and realism, between classicism and romanticism, flared up at the Paris Salon of 1822, at which Delacroix, who was to play a unique role in the history of watercolour painting, exhibited his painting *Dante and Virgil Crossing the Styx*, and an English friend of Géricault, Richard Parkes Bonington, showed two simple watercolours of landscapes in Normandy, which caused a sensation. Beside these works, the conventional historico-literary paintings on the walls appeared already moribund. Géricault himself had already visited England and brought back glowing accounts, but it was only now that the younger generation of French artists began to realize that English artists were already achieving something that had so far eluded them, that 'something' which in France was the subject only of the boldest imaginings, was already taken for granted in England: nature itself, the boundlessness of the atmosphere, freedom of content. A successful campaign was launched to invite a group of English artists, including the leading watercolourists, to exhibit at the 1824 Salon. In spite of the critical indignation of the general public, Delacroix voiced the enthusiasm of the young French painters: 'Air! Space! Diamonds that flatter and ravish the eye, irrespective of subject and imitation!' This exhibition marked the start of the immeasurable influence that Constable was to exercise over French painting. Although critics complained that the *Hay Wain* looked as if the artist had thrown a paint-soaked sponge at the canvas, Delacroix was so inspired by it that he repainted the landscape sections of his own *Massacre at Chios*, which he had already submitted to the same exhibition. Constable himself was astonished by the enthusiasm, which was far stronger than it ever was in England. He had written to a friend that French artists knew as much about nature as a cab-horse did of meadows; 'they neglect the look of nature altogether, under its various changes.' It was Delacroix again who recognized that light breaks objects up into coloured reflections, and that the only way to do justice to the shimmering world of appearances was to use colours unmixed: 'It is best not to mix spots of colour physically. They mix naturally when seen from a distance, according to the law of sympathy that brings them together.' This fact was not to be exploited systematically until much later.

The dynamism of Romantic art made it especially susceptible to one preoccupation which, for Constable particularly was an obsession: the effort to do justice to the constantly changing appearance of nature – 'No two days are alike, nor even two hours', he said. Theme and literary content, intellectual communication, even spiritual elevation or patriotic emotion receded in importance and the work of art for its own sake became paramount; instead of the means it now became the end. As a result, the object depicted had to be as devoid of significance as possible, and, instead of attempting to represent something complete in itself, a landscape had as far as possible to be a random section of a scene. Only in circumstances like these did it become possible to demonstrate the changes in light and atmosphere which now became the subject of painting. The artist had to work spontaneously, in full sight of the changes in nature as they occurred in order to capture their immediacy. It was an enterprise that cried out for watercolour, and the use of watercolour by Romantic artists (cf. Delacroix's sketchbook of his travels in North Africa, *pl. XI*) brought about a striking resurgence in its fortunes.

Boudin to Cézanne

Following his success at the Paris Salon of 1822 Bonington exhibited some seascapes at the Salon of 1824. These established marine painting in watercolour as an independent genre and the shimmer and sheen of the water, the gentle haze over picturesque harbours and the busy gaiety of beaches were to preoccupy, if not always to inspire generations of French painters. Eugène Isabey (1804–86), the son of the miniaturist, devoted himself entirely to seascapes, weighing his compositions down with rather self-conscious genre and historical themes when painting in oils, but revealing himself as a master of lightness and speed in his watercolours, which are unsurpassed in the rendering of colours and light-effects in the spray and swirl of green water. The most interesting of the French marine artists however is Eugène Boudin (1824–98) who did most of his work on the Seine estuary. Baudelaire describes how Boudin made a note on every sketch of the date, the time of day and the state of the weather, so that he could register the changes in the atmosphere, and Boudin himself constantly stressed the importance of working out of doors: 'We do not represent the world so much as the element that enfolds it.' Boudin's work was one of the sources of the inspiration of the early impressionists. 'I try again and again from the beginning to capture this magic of the light which is everywhere ... The objects are submerged, there exist only values.' These values could not be imagined by the artist in his studio, they had to be seen in the open air. 'Three strokes of the brush from nature are worth more than two days' work indoors; everything that is painted directly has a power and vitality which cannot be obtained in any other way.' These theories were unconventional and totally unacceptable in academies, but they had a strong direct influence on Monet, whom Boudin introduced to landscape painting in 1862 in Le Havre, and on Jongkind. Johan Barthold Jongkind (1819–91), whose life was a disaster ending in madness, and whose work viewed as a whole is very uneven, produced watercolours which are among the loveliest ever painted. No other artist has equalled the pregnant immediacy with which he endowed even the most fleeting of sensory perceptions, or the fluency of his *écriture rapide*. His method of applying patches of colour with a relaxed, loaded brush was one of the impressionists' formative influences.

The impressionists were also influenced, albeit indirectly, by the realistic landscapes of the Barbizon School, a group of painters centred on a village in the Forest of Fontainebleau. Its members, who included Millet, Théodore Rousseau, Diaz, Jaques, Troyon, Daubigny and, later, Boudin, felt an instinctive sympathy with the simple undramatic landscape of the area which they rendered in 'paysages intimes'. Sketching directly from nature they sought, as Constable had done, to render nature not as it was thought to be but as it was, and it was this realism that affected Corot and Courbet.

Landscape was not however the only field in which watercolour's properties were especially appropriate. Its suitability for making rapid, on-the-spot records of impressions or events also made it attractive to genre painters and particularly to satirists and critics of society, whose concern was to capture on paper a situation, a pose or a gesture of an instant's duration. The primary medium of the greatest social critic of all, Honoré Daumier (1808–79), was line drawing, but he painted a small number of landscapes in watercolour which are among the best of their kind. They are full of life and warm colour and their mood of reconciliation suggests that Daumier found nature a refuge when the strain of his chosen role as prosecutor of human deceits threatened to overwhelm him.

Since so much of Daumier's work was overtly or covertly satirical it seems misleading to include him among the *chroniqueurs*, so called for their faithful, vivid and slightly romanticized chronicle of life under the Second Empire. The paintings of Eugène Lami and Gavarni are typical of the group in the finesse and charm with which they depict the Paris of their day. Eugène Lami (1800–90) has been credited with the invention of *gouache-aquarelle*, but a 'semi-opaque' technique was practised by the Norwich School and by Cotman himself by 1830, and Menzel began to use his similar mixture of media at much the same date and with far more worthwhile results. In a wider sense, French painters of military subjects were also *chroniqueurs*, artists like Charlet and Raffet who nostalgically recalled the *Grande Armée*, or Edouard Detaille, who recorded the ideals of military honour and patriotism of the Franco-Prussian war in the grand manner of a history painter.

Most of the *chroniqueurs* were also excellent watercolourists but none received anything like the admiration which fell to Ernest Meissonier (1815–91), who for half a century was acclaimed as a 'god of academic art', only to be completely forgotten very soon after his death. He has recently found renewed recognition – Salvador Dali believes he should be ranked above Cézanne. Meissonier unquestionably possessed a peerless technical perfection in all fields:

history painting, genre, portraiture and landscape. Like Menzel he recognized the previously unsuspected potentialities of mixing gouache and transparent watercolour; a work executed in such a mixture could make an effect very like that of oil, which made it attractive to the new middle class as something to hang on its own walls. Its technical advantages to the artist were clear: the ability to achieve rich, dense lights and shadows impossible with the delicate transparency of pure watercolour; the heightened immediacy created by an area of blank paper amid the strength of the colours; and the range of incredibly refined effects obtainable by exploiting textural properties, the roughness of the paper, the effect of dabbing at the moist paint with the brush, or even scratching away colour already applied to give a highlight. It is easy to understand the general chorus of praise for Meissonier; there is no denying the virtuosity and brilliance in his depiction of a world of nobility, elegance and pathos, the world of his public's dreams.

Meissonier was succeeded by generations of virtuosi, particularly in Italy and Spain. Four Italian watercolourists who went on working to the end of the century, Alessandro Durini, Eleuterio Pagliano, Carlo Mancini and Tranquillo Cremona, were artists of considerable stature, although Serafino Ricci's assessment of them in 1912 as *valentissime forsi insuperabile* probably overstates the case. By contrast with theirs, the work of Constantin Guys (1802–92), the likeable portrayer of *la vie parisienne*, might seem a little colourless, suffering from a certain uniformity of subject: the crinolined ladies of his day strolling on the boulevards or seated gracefully in boxes at the Opéra and in cafés. But Guys's expressive ability is of a higher order than appears at first glance. That Baudelaire chose to write a long essay about him should surprise nobody, for human anxieties lurk behind the masks of charm and unconcern. Though his colouring is rather limited in its range, the way he raises his china-doll figures from individual to general significance perhaps says more about the Second Empire than all the anecdotes and social histories put together.

The major artistic advance of the second half of the nineteenth century was made, however, not by the *chroniqueurs* and their like, but by a small, despised group – the impressionists. It has already been suggested that in some respects both the romantics and the Barbizon School of landscape painting were the precursors of impressionism, and the two influences join together in Courbet's peremptory injunction to his pupils: 'Paint what you see!' In 1855 Camille

Pissarro (1831–1903) arrived in Paris, determined to follow in the footsteps of Delacroix and Courbet. In 1861 he met Cézanne and Guillaumin, both still students, and soon afterwards made the acquaintance of Monet, who was already friendly with Renoir, Sisley and Bazille. Claude Monet (1840–1926) had met Boudin in 1858 and worked with him and Jongkind on the coast at Le Havre in 1862 and was therefore far in advance of his friends as a landscape painter. He, too, is said to have studied nothing in nature but colour values, but he goes further in his statement: 'Painting is nothing more than an experiment with effects of light and shade!' This means virtually the same as a famous saying of Corot: 'Let us surrender ourselves to the impression!'

The problem facing the impressionists was that of combining colours to create a total effect and their goal the depiction of visible phenomena with optical realism. The initial reactions of the public were incomprehension and hostility. The group gave eight exhibitions of their work between 1874 and 1886, arousing scandal and dissension. The derisive term 'impressionist' was coined by the critic Louis Leroy who described the paintings on view at the first exhibition as 'a smear of colours'. The 'smear', however, achieved international acclaim within twelve years, scoring a triumph in New York in the same year as the last of the Paris exhibitions. That impressionist paintings could be described in such terms was due to a fundamental misapprehension and distrust of the impressionist technique of breaking down the forms of objects into little dabs of pure colour which are only united when the painting is viewed from a certain distance away. The technique was based on an understanding of the nature of the spectrum, of the effect of juxtaposing contrasting colours instead of mixing them, and the significance of complementary colours.

The impressionists' prime concern, however, was not with the technique as an end in itself, but as a means to convey actual experience, to record the effect of light, whether a soft shimmer or a brilliant glare, on a scene in nature, and clearly watercolour's ability to record first impressions must have been especially valuable to them in this. All the major impressionists, Monet – who had been greatly influenced by Turner when he visited London in 1870–71 – Manet, Renoir and Sisley painted remarkably beautiful, radiant watercolours, free, luminous visions dressed in clear, delicate colours (*pls. XIII, XIV, 24*).

The last impressionist group showing was held in 1886. By then Seurat and Signac had already struck out in the direction of neo-impressionism, which was based on scientific principles of colour. Earlier experiments by various physicists, Sutter, Blanc, Roos and Chevreuil among others, had resulted in the conclusion that no kind of 'subtractive' mixing of colours (that is, a mixture made on the palette or in water) was capable of producing the intensity of colour as perceived by the eye; the only way to do it was by juxtaposing dots and dabs of the colours of the spectrum. 'The mixture of pigments must be replaced by optical mixture,' said Pissarro in 1885, expressing his enthusiasm, which was not shared by all the impressionists, for the physico-scientific technique of Georges Seurat (1859–91). Seurat's most devoted follower and an important figure in the neo-impressionist movement was Paul Signac. Signac travelled widely throughout his life and painted innumerable sketches and watercolours as preliminary studies for oil-paintings (*pl. XV*). His book *D'Eugène Delacroix au néo-impressionnisme* is an important guide to the movement, which had by then, however, reached a dead end. The second leading watercolourist of the period, Henri Edmond Cross, had also joined Seurat's neo-impressionist camp, and there were others who were more extreme in their pointillism, Hippolyte Petitjean for instance, and who took the principle of additive colour as far as they could in watercolour painting.

While impressionism was causing such a stir, another artist with a totally different view of the world was almost completely ignored by his contemporaries. Gustave Moreau was little known in his lifetime and immediately forgotten on his death; interest in him can really be said to date only from 1961, although André Breton had recognized the subliminal validity of his work before that and both the symbolists and the surrealists had adopted some features of his morbid visions and bizarre mysticism, which owe something to Turner (*pl. XII*).

Moreau earned his living as a teacher; his pupils included Henri Matisse and Albert Marquet, as well as Georges Rouault. Rouault's career led him out of Moreau's esoteric world into a profound and penetrating realism for a time (*pl. 27*); he overcame this and in his protest against the terrors of desolation and human loneliness in the modern world he became the greatest religious painter of the twentieth century. Some of the principles instilled by Moreau still lie, however, at the base of his fauvism: 'I do not believe in the truth either of what I touch, or of what I see, but only in my instinct.' He believed that the artist must conceive colours in his mind before painting them, in this making common cause with

Gauguin's rejection of impressionism: 'All this mess of authentic colours is a lifeless, frozen lie.' In the last analysis, even Van Gogh's 'suggestive' colours, with their aggressive and expressive formal power, are drawn from the same inner source.

The Nabis, a group of French symbolist artists active from 1889 to 1899, had already broken with impressionism; their spokesman Maurice Denis gave the ultimate definition of a picture as 'a flat surface covered with colours assembled in a certain order'. Watercolour's small format and subtle brushwork was ill-suited to this approach, yet it was at this moment in time that the medium reached its zenith, in the work of Cézanne.

Paul Cézanne (1839–1906) did not keep company with the impressionists for very long. He became convinced that the truth of nature did not lie on its surface but far deeper, in elemental forces. Colour was only the surface expression of these depths, and in seizing the impressions of colour – which was the only way to define painting – the artist was not copying the object but recognizing the truth, the essence, which had an endurance and significance far above that of the momentary impression. 'We have only to make its eternity visible!' he said. Cézanne painted slowly and carefully, continually checking his work by looking at nature. The sensitivity with which he probed the relationships and contrasts of colours was inexhaustible. Just as important as his recognition of the fundamental shapes of the cylinder, the sphere and the cone behind the forms of nature, which laid the foundations for cubism, was his understanding of the essentially formal qualities of colours, which could be exploited in a completely new way. Notwithstanding the power of his brush in oils, in watercolour he was capable of extraordinarily delicate nuances. For all its tonal richness, the colouring is often reduced to tiny tentative dabs of yellow and red with blue shadows, but this is enough to give the work a structural clarity, an inner form which creates a monumental effect. The highest form of discipline is to recreate the essence of an object by knowing the exact moment when to stop painting and in Cézanne's work the white parts of a watercolour are no longer areas that have been forgotten or left blank but have become structural elements in the composition. Cézanne never ceased to paint specific subjects, such as the scenery of Provence or still-lifes, the permanence and immobility of which was particularly suited to his purposes (*pls. I, 25*). The picture, the construction on the painting surface, was for him an independent organism, a microcosm. His own purpose was always to convey sensations, but others learned from him something rather different: perception of innermost truths about the visible world. He thus completely broke the spell of impressionism. 'The magic of the present and instantaneous turned into the mystery of the permanent and the eternal, vibrant, humming life becomes resounding stillness' (F. Novotny). Cézanne gave the world a new way of seeing.

13 JEAN-HONORÉ FRAGONARD (Grasse 1732–1806 Paris)
The Embrace. Bistre wash, black chalk. 455: 310 mm. Albertina, Vienna. Inv. 12,726.
The stone plaque bears the inscription *Spirat adhuc Amor* ('Love still lives') from Horace, *Odes* IV, 9. This is a study for a painting which has been lost (though an engraving of it by the Comte de Paroy survives). A magnificent example of chiaroscuro.

14 JEAN-BAPTISTE ISABEY (Nancy 1767–1855 Paris)
Archduke Charles. 1812. Watercolour. 137:100 mm. (oval). Albertina, Vienna. Inv. 34,659.
One of a series of sixteen portraits of members of the Imperial family, commissioned by Napoleon for Marie Louise.

15 JOSEF DANHAUSER (Vienna 1805–45)
Girl in a Poke Bonnet. Wash over faint drawing. 217:187 mm. Albertina, Vienna. Inv. 26,704.
The delicacy of watercolour is ideally suited to the depiction of the agreeable society of the Biedermeier period. The young woman in the fashionable yellow hat is Danhauser's wife, Josephine.

16 FRANÇOIS DUMONT (Lunéville 1751–1831 Paris)
Countess Elisabeth Rasumovska. 1795. Watercolour and gouache on ivory. Diameter: 72 mm. L.S. collection, London and Vienna.
French rococo miniature painting continued to flourish, *mutatis mutandis*, after 1789.

17 JOHANN GRUND (Vienna 1808–87 Baden-Baden)
Portrait of the Artist's First Wife. 1831. Watercolour with gouache highlights. 139:111 mm. Staatliche Kunsthalle, Karlsruhe. Inv. 1939–6.
The artist has used his brush with great delicacy to portray the charm and sincerity of his young wife.

18 RUDOLF VON ALT (Vienna 1812–1905)
The Dumba Family. Watercolour. 207:270 mm. Anton Schmid collection, Vienna.
Alt spend the month of September 1879 on the country estate of Nikolaus von Dumba, banker and patron of the arts, at Liezen. This colourful, spontaneous sketch, painted on a picnic, displays the full, free range of his brush.

19 KARL ROTTMANN (Handschuhsheim 1797–1850 Munich)
Marathon. Wash over pencil drawing. 288:383 mm. Staatliche Graphische Sammlung, Munich. Inv. 21,386.
One of the series of historic sites in Italy and Greece painted 1826–27 on a commission from King Ludwig I. The thunderstorm brewing over the lonely bay echoes, in the late Romantic manner, the drama of the battle of 490 BC, which changed the history of the world.

20 ERNST FRIES (Heidelberg 1801–33 Karlsruhe)
The Park of the Villa Chigi, Ariccia. Watercolour. 388:535 mm. Staatliche Kunsthalle, Karlsruhe. Inv. VIII, 1380.
Fries and Ludwig Richter visited 'this magic forest out of a fairy tale, which surpasses all one's most vivid fantasies' in the spring of 1824.

21 WINSLOW HOMER (Boston, Massachusetts 1836–1910 Prout's Neck, Maine)
Shooting the Rapids. 1897. Watercolour. 343: 521 mm. Fogg Art Museum, Cambridge, Mass.
From 1895 on, when he was at the height of his powers, Homer spent every summer among lumberjacks in the vast natural solitude of Lake Tourilli in Quebec province. The series of watercolours he painted there were the foundation of his greatest successes.

13

14

15

16

17

Familie Kümpel   Skizze von Rudolf v. Ott
                                  bestätigt Louise v. Ott

18

19

20

21

22

23

24

22 PETER FENDI (Vienna 1796–1842)
The Daughters of the Prince of Liechtenstein. 1833. Wash over faint pencil drawing. 196:234 mm. Albertina, Vienna. Inv. 31,016.

This depicts the two young princesses Elise and Fanny, later Princess Salm-Reifferscheidt-Raitz and Princess Arenberg, with their governess.

23 CARL BLECHEN (Cottbus 1798–1840 Berlin)
Ruined Gothic Church. Wash over traces of pencil drawing. 373:259 mm. Nationalgalerie, Berlin. NG 562 (*Werkskatalog* No. 1884).

Romantic artists were especially attracted by the atmosphere of monastic ruins in dense forests. Blechen painted a number of works with similar subjects around 1831.

24 ÉDOUARD MANET (Paris 1832–83)
Flowerpiece with Golden Rain and Irises. Watercolour. 351:256 mm. Albertina, Vienna. Inv. 24,129. Manet's flower still-lifes, painted in soft, transparent colours, depict light as the essence of a reality which loses its material character when it is illuminated.

Twentieth-Century Currents
in Europe and the United States

Cézanne is the key figure in the period of transition to the art of our day and age. As his theories became widely known, so did his technique, in which the relationship between one area of colour and the next is reduced to the simple complementary tensions of local colours. This principle became accepted all over Europe.

By this time, however, Europe's monopoly of 'Western' art had been challenged from the United States. The first painter to create truly American works was probably Winslow Homer (1836–1910) (*pl. 21*); before him, the only American artists who received attention were those who lived and worked in Europe: Whistler, Benjamin West and John Singleton Copley. Homer was the first to develop a vigorously realistic, indigenous painting, taking the American scene as his subject. As it did in Europe, the art of watercolour painting in America arose jointly from the practice of tinting engravings and from its use in the recording of natural phenomena, as for instance in the work of the ornithologist John James Audubon. This was the source of the belief that the faithful reproduction was not only possible but necessary, which was the basic principle of the Hudson River School. Homer struck a more independent line from 1873 onwards, actually painting his watercolours in the open air. At the age of forty-seven he withdrew to the lonely coast of Maine, to paint the simple, outdoor lives of lumberjacks and fishermen. Later he travelled in Florida and the Caribbean, where he discovered a quite different world, rich in colours, which made him the most considerable artistic force in his generation. Before Homer, watercolour in America was a technique for amateurs, professional artists using it only in the preparatory stages of oil-paintings, but he raised it to equality with all the other media. A whole series of artists followed his lead, notably his near-contemporary Thomas Eakins (1844–1916), who also combined his painting activities at the Pennsylvania Academy of Fine Arts with an open-air life and, in a relatively short period, between 1870 and 1880, produced some excellent work in watercolour. Eakins had one extraordinary foible: he used oils in preliminary studies and sketches for paintings which he executed in watercolour.

The artistic events of our own century are still too close for us to be able to assess their historical importance, but certain trends and their origins are quite clear. The influence of the Far East, in particular, was already discernible before the end of the nineteenth century. A series of trade agreements, beginning in 1853, had brought Japan into contact with the rest of the world, first with the United States and later with England, France and Russia. Examples of Japanese art, notably coloured woodcuts, were shown at the international exhibition of 1862 in London, and aroused the greatest interest then and at subsequent exhibitions, in Paris in 1867 and in Vienna in 1873. Fascinated, artists adopted the new forms, themes and principles especially the ornamental arrangement of the surface of the painting, the calligraphic line and the bird's-eye view, and the renewed use of the woodcut in Europe is directly attributable to the Japanese influence.

Another immensely important figure in the years after 1890 was that of the great Scandinavian, Edvard Munch, whose work epitomizes our idea of the *fin de siècle*. Always extremely personal, his painting is possessed by a unique, despairing poetry of suffering and existentialist *Angst* until about 1907 when lightness, nature and optimism begin to assert themselves. His finest watercolours date from this later period.

Art Nouveau was far from pessimistic; it was the positive expression of revolt against stagnant traditions and historicism, it was a hopeful quest for new ideals. This pan-European movement was centred on Vienna and Austria was at that time at the crest of an artistic and social renaissance to which philosophers, poets, composers, doctors, men of science and of the arts, all made positive contributions. Developments in the visual arts were dominated by Gustav Klimt (1862–1918), who in 1898 founded a group called the Vienna Secession. The young artists of his circle faced existence with an ecstatic empathy, believing that art would usher in a sacred spring – *Ver sacrum* was the name they gave to their journal. Their motto can still be read on the façade of the exhibition centre of the Vienna Secession: *Der Zeit ihre Kunst, der Kunst ihre Freiheit* ('to the age its art, to art its freedom'). Klimt himself never worked in watercolour, but the aged Rudolf von Alt, still active in the medium, was elected the honorary president of the Secession. All the young artists revered him for his open-minded approach to all new ideas, and there was not one who did not try to emulate his brush technique. In the early days of the Secession, however, the most notable achievements were in other media, in pen-and-ink drawing, or in gouache.

Klimt left the Secession in 1905, in pursuit of an art that would penetrate every aspect of life. It was in support of this aim that he organized the great *Kunstschau* exhibition of modern art in Vienna in 1908, which included works by two very young men who were to become two of the greatest artists of the century: Egon Schiele (1890–1918) and Oskar Kokoschka. The artistic environment in which they grew up is the only thing the two had in common. At eighteen Schiele already had a new and terrifying experience of the fundamentals of existence. Menaced by the environment, fate and the ego, he was incapable of depicting a world of beautiful inspirations and symbolic appearances; his work documents a tormented passion to interpret and subjugate, to counter 'existence unto death' with the power of the creative process. Apart from the early works of 1910, most of his watercolours are in fact painted in heavily-thinned gouache or sometimes even in tempera, and are dominated visually by the explosive force of the line drawing. Kokoschka on the other hand has turned to pure watercolour at two quite distinct periods in his life. Some of the studies for the *Dreaming Boys* and the nudes of 1912–13 were probably coloured, but the first significant use of transparent watercolour was in his Dresden period, 1917–24. The portraits and figures of the early twenties are true masterpieces, painted with broad strokes of the brush in pale, almost neutral colours, that achieve the utmost of expressive force (*pl. 30*). Thirty years later Kokoschka began to use watercolour again, this time in landscapes, still-lifes and flower pieces, delicately coloured compositions which are among the finest of his later works.

In France, meanwhile, an artistic revolution had been taking place. The decisive reaction against the 'tyranny of divisionism', imposed by Seurat and his followers, came in 1905, with an exhibition of works by Henri Matisse, Georges Rouault, Henri Manguin, André Derain and Maurice Vlaminck that were so radically new that they earned their painters the title of 'les fauves' ('the wild ones'). Albert Marquet and Kees van Dongen soon joined these revolutionaries who wanted the process of creation to mean surrendering to passion and instinct, and painting to be released from the bonds of theory, symbolism, allegory and history; they wanted a fresh, naive vision of the world, like a child's, and they sought to give their motifs intrinsic vitality and force by 'translation into heightened, simple, pure surface values of colour and line' (Matisse: *Notes d'un peintre* 1908).

The role they assigned to watercolour was a completely new one: chromatic aggression. Orgies of colour were unleashed, by Matisse, who evolved

XIII CAMILLE PISSARRO (Saint-Thomas 1831–1903 Paris).
The Funeral of Cardinal Bonnechose in Rouen. Watercolour. 228:298 mm. Louvre, Paris.
From 1872 Pissarro gathered about him a group of young artists, including Cézanne, who allied themselves to the impressionist cause, under his leadership. In this painting he depicts the innumerable throng of the mourners as a solid, dark wall, while the funeral procession itself is fused into a single sombre unit.

XIV AUGUSTE RENOIR (Limoges 1841–1919 Cagnes).
River Scene. 1890. Watercolour. 253:338 mm. Albertina, Vienna. Inv. 24.112.
Renoir's journey to Italy in 1881 was a turning-point in Renoir's development. His experience of the work of Raphael and the Italian primitives deflected him from impressionism. Around 1890, however, he reverted to soft, painterly forms and to delicate merging of tones, achieved by overlaying the brush strokes.

Rouen, enterrement du Cardinal B...

XIII

XV

XVI

a style of arabesque surfaces, by Raoul Dufy in paintings of radiant freshness, whose chromatic harmonies reveal the transparency of the medium as hardly any other artist has ever done, by Vlaminck, who shaped incandescent landscapes from violent contrasts, and by Van Dongen, one of the most remarkable of them all, whose brilliant paintings combine a passion for life with acute powers of observation.

The fauves were deposed in their turn. Pablo Picasso and Georges Braque embarked on a radical simplification of elements, and through geometricization of the physical world arrived at the first principle of cubism and the beginning of a new era in the history of art. The primary goal of the cubists was to create a multi-faceted form to set up as a mirror to the unknown essence of the object; the concept of the *peinture-objet* crystallized, imbued with a fundamental autonomy that the *nature-objet* lacked. Earlier in his career Picasso had used watercolour and he was to revert to it occasionally later, but in the early days of cubism, like Braque and Gris, he largely abandoned colour for brown or grey monochrome.

In *Les peintres cubistes*, 1913, Apollinaire expounded the theory that it was not the concern of painting to imitate what nature had already created quite adequately, but that instead it must realize its potential for creating new realities; fusions of forms and colours on the painting surface could construct imaginary spaces and undreamt-of expanses. 'As long as art does not free itself from the object, it is condemned by its own hand to slavery.'

The influence that theories like these had on artists working in Germany, such as Klee, Marc and Macke should not be underestimated. It was only a relatively short time since social circumstances in Germany had entrenched academicism, which took the form of grandiose history painting, more firmly there than in any other country. Art had become a substitute religion, the muses were invoked as the inspiration of a mood of earnest dedication; even impressionism was deemed to be radicalism of extreme temerity. The liberation of colour was pioneered by three painters: Max Slevogt, whose

XV PAUL SIGNAC (Paris 1863–1935).
Constantinople. 1907. Watercolour over drawing. 270:403 mm. Staatliche Kunstsammlungen, Schloßmuseum, Weimar.
His preoccupation with theories of light and optics and his acquaintance with Seurat led Signac to join the group of artists to whom he himself gave the pragmatic title of 'Chromoluminarists'. Light is represented by the purely painterly technique of leaving the paper blank in the interstices between the brush strokes.

XVI LOVIS CORINTH (Tapiau 1858–1925 Zandvoort).
Self-portrait. 1921. Watercolour. 392:285 mm. Städtische Sammlungen, Ulm.
This is the culmination of a series of self-portraits: the dissolution of rigid forms, the intensification of colours that have been reduced to their essentials, and the positioning of the massive face on the surface, give it a visionary power.

narrative invention gave his work tremendous vitality; Max Liebermann; and Lovis Corinth, whose landscapes of the Walchensee, painted in the 1920s, represent the zenith of German impressionism.

But a revolution of far greater importance had burst upon Germany in the very first years of the century. While the fauves and the cubists were primarily concerned with form and structure, expressionism swept away all conventional colour harmonies in an eruption of colour and form welling up from the artist's innermost being with a violence and spontaneity that made a direct emotional appeal to the spectator. Painting in watercolours now took on a function quite unlike any it had ever known and achieved an unprecedented power through the use of strong patches of local colour; as Werner Hofmann says, 'the expansive spot of colour takes on its maximal measure of quicksilvery life and vital pleasure when paired with another.' This new role for watercolour was devised by Ernst Ludwig Kirchner who, with Erich Heckel and Karl Schmidt-Rottluff formed *Die Brücke* in Dresden in 1904. Kirchner, who as the oldest was also the leader of the group, insisted on the all-important release that was to be obtained from the experience of nature: 'For me nature is everything visible and everything tangible in the world, the mountain and the atom, the tree and the cells that go to construct it, but also everything made by man, like machines.' Kirchner's watercolour painting reached a peak in his views of Berlin. Expressionist colouring was very strongly influenced by Delaunay's essay on light, (which Klee translated into German in 1913) in which he claimed that all art is polyrhythmia, a harmony of colours which simultaneously separate and come together again as a whole. The artists of *Die Brücke*, however, were not concerned with capturing the impression of reality but with a new purpose: a work of art should reflect the picture that springs up in the human spirit in response to, and as a result of experiences and intuitions of nature and life. As modern art developed along these lines, no other medium played such a sustaining role as watercolour – which was yet doing no more than fulfil its essential nature by creating chromatic harmonies with untrammelled spontaneity.

Another radical group, *Der Blaue Reiter*, was formed in Munich in 1911 by the two Russians, Wassily Kandinsky and Alexey von Jawlensky, who were deeply influenced by fauvism, and Franz Marc, August Macke and Paul Klee. The resulting group was profoundly influenced by the aesthetic theories of Otto Fischer: 'Colour is a medium of expression which speaks directly to the soul. Colour is a medium of composition. Things are more than things when they are the expression of the soul.' Kandinsky's own theoretical writing (*Concerning the Spiritual in Art*, published in Munich in 1912) demonstrates the intellectual level of their deliberations.

Shortly before the outbreak of war, Macke and Klee went to Kairouan in

Tunisia. The watercolours that Macke painted there – more than thirty-seven of them – were to be his last works and constitute one of summits of European art, although some were destroyed under the Third Reich as 'degenerate art' (*pl. XX*). It was in Tunisia, too, that Klee made his momentous personal discovery of colour, while working in watercolour. His diary records it: 'Colour possesses me ... That is the whole meaning of this happy hour. Colour and I are one' (16 April 1914). 'Departure from Tunis ... Many watercolours and all sorts of other things. Most of it inside me, deep inside, but I'm so full that it keeps bubbling out' (19 April 1914). It was as though the crystal of which Delaunay wrote, in which transparent colours penetrate each other like rays of light, now found its ultimate realization.

From this time on Klee's range of expression was extended by his use of watercolour. Even greater possibilities were opened up by the technical innovations and enrichment of all the artistic media at the Bauhaus, the art school founded at Weimar in 1919 by the architect Walter Gropius, at which Klee and Kandinsky later became teachers. These included completely new effects obtained by spattering the paint on to the picture surface, and by the use of stencils and stereotypes. With a more relaxed style, Klee was able to develop a synthesis of sensual and extra-sensual perceptual images (*pl. XVIII*).

The first abstract picture, painted by Wassily Kandinsky in 1910, was a watercolour. Kandinsky later explained what drew him to abstraction: it was not the actual process of 'abstracting', the simplifying or deforming of an object, nor yet any desire to compose a visual counterpoint of forms in accordance with his belief in the analogy between colours and musical sounds; it was that, while experimenting with watercolour, he came to recognize what theorists had already posited, that colour and form were able to set up a powerful resonance in the human soul, and that this resonance was bound to be even stronger if the eye was not distracted by the associations clinging to particular objects. 'So at last I entered the kingdom of art which, like the kingdoms of nature and science, like political entities, is an independent realm, governed by its own unique laws, and which ultimately unites with the others to form that great kingdom of which we are only dimly aware' (*pl. 29*).

Of the other great watercolourists who were members of the Bauhaus, the American-born Lyonel Feininger at least must be mentioned. His sensitive, crystalline studies are predominantly concerned with line and form, but after 1924, when he settled in the village of Deep in Pomerania, he began to paint the series of watercolours of shipping, distinguished by their delicate colouring, which are among his finest, most poetic works (*pl. XIX*).

No other artist of our time has been so steadfast in his devotion to watercolour as Emil Nolde. He began to use the medium in 1895, laying the paint on the paper in large blobs, and had his first successes during his period in Switzerland. In his early flower studies of 1906–08 he used the brush as a drawing implement, but soon mastered the technique of overpainting while the preceding wash was still wet, using very absorbent Japanese paper, and by the time he reached the height of his powers in the 1920s he had no equal working in the medium. Nolde had already shown himself capable of some remarkable effects in his views of Berlin of 1910–11 by drying the edges of areas of paint, a technique he developed further during his travels in Polynesia; at the end of his life he drew together all the threads of his knowledge and experience in the so-called *Unpainted pictures*, executed during World War II when, forbidden to paint by the Nazi regime, he went into hiding at his house at Seebüll near the Danish border (*pl. XVII*). Although most of his visions of gnomes, monsters and phantoms are in body colour, at Seebüll, year after year, Nolde also painted lovely flower studies in pure watercolour. In 1942 he wrote in his notebook, 'Flowers bloom to give people joy; I paint them in summer and prolong the joy into winter.'

The trend to various forms of expressionistic painting in the first decades of this century was an international one. In America, John Marin formulated a very personal and striking view of the urban landscape, depicting the ebb and flow of human masses and convulsive, overlapping lines of spatial relationships – Hofmann speaks of 'his resolve to break up his formal structures dynamically'. Marin made his personal conquest of all forms of traditionalism in a series of watercolours which he painted as early as 1909, while travelling in the Tyrol. His skill in watercolour is also amply demonstrated by the studies he painted summer after summer at Cape Split on the coast of Maine (*pl. XXII*). He must have been exposed to some powerful impressions, particularly in Paris, during his years in Europe from 1905 to 1911, but it was not until his return to the United States, and apparently quite independently of all influences, that he first attained maturity – above all in watercolour. He did not begin to paint in oils until after 1925.

Many American painters explored the uses of watercolour: Charles Demuth (1883–1935), whose sensitive paintings combine intensity of colour with complete technical mastery; Edward Hopper (1882–1967), who took up

XVII EMIL NOLDE (Nolde 1867–1956 Seebüll).
The Sea (*Violet, Yellow, Green*). Watercolour. 339:472 mm. Stiftung Ada und Emil Nolde, Seebüll.
Watercolour was the medium in which Nolde was able to express himself most powerfully from about 1888 onwards. From 1908 he began to use the technique of applying paint while previous washes were still wet, so that the colours merged on the paper, which he held to be a 'collaboration of nature'. *The Sea* is a late work, probably *c.* 1945, and employs only the two primary colours, yellow and blue, from which Nolde was also able to obtain all the nuances of green by overpainting.

XVII

1922/ 69.   Der Bote des Herbstes

XVIII

watercolour in 1923; Maurice Prendergast (1859–1924), a post-impressionist who evolved particularly sensitive colouristic values; and finally Morris Graves and Reginald Marsh. But the tendency in America has been increasingly towards large dimensions and to painting huge expanses of opaque, undifferentiated colour. The abstract expressionists Jackson Pollock and Mark Tobey had no use for watercolour; Mark Rothko, Franz Kline and Willem de Kooning, very little or none, though Sam Francis occasionally uses transparent watercolours in his dynamic improvisations such as *Structure No. 2* in the Metropolitan Museum of Art, New York. Although watercolour has no place whatever in the current pop, op and minimal art movements, its tradition is brilliantly continued by artists such as Andrew Wyeth, who has made incisive studies in pure watercolour, although he works most often in gouache and tempera.

The year 1918 marked a great divide in European art, which was deepened in Austria by the deaths of both Klimt and Schiele. Since that time Austria has produced a number of fine watercolourists. Wilhelm Thöny, who reached his peak around 1935, at a time when he was equally fascinated by Paris and New York, was a painter and graphic artist of great originality, intelligence and culture (*pl. XXIII*). Herbert Boeckl possessed a personality of both depth and force, as well as unparalleled technical facility; the different periods in his career are signposted by his use of different techniques. He reached an early peak in watercolour in the late 1920s and another after 1949 in the *Metamorphoses*, a late and original cycle in which he began by exploring chromatic relationships of visionary tenderness and went on to ever freer interpretation and transformation of the same landscape subject. Kurt Absolon (1925–58), in his short life, demonstrated an extreme sensitivity in paintings of unusual expressiveness and density. Finally, Kurt Moldovan's most recent watercolours are among the best of the present day.

In Italy, after the brief but dramatic reign of futurism, something not dissimilar to cubism evolved, but holding rather different aims. Simultaneity was the watchword, meaning the simultaneous depiction of things that were actually sequential – in other words the suspension of the movement of time. The solid surface character of gouache was decidedly more suited to such an undertaking than watercolour. The great innovators, Carlo Carrà, Umberto Boccioni, Arturo Tosi and Ardengo Soffici, and later the

XVIII PAUL KLEE (Münchenbuchsee, Berne 1879–1940 Muralto, Locarno).
The Herald of Autumn. 1922. Watercolour. 264:322 mm. Yale University Art Gallery, New Haven, Conn.
The cool, muted nuances of greys, violets and greens, arranged in clear, rectangular facets, provide the strongest possible contrast to the isolated tree in autumnal orange.

25 PAUL CÉZANNE (Aix-en-Provence 1839–1906)
The Balcony. Wash over pencil drawing. 550: 390 mm. Philadelphia Museum of Art, Philadelphia.
Cézanne constantly aspired to insight into nature. His view from a balcony, the human vantage point, into the impenetrable Opposite of the world in the background of the painting, reveals the inner forces of nature. 'There is more of nature in the depths than on the surface; colours are an expression of these depths, they rise up out of the roots of the world.'

26 HENRI DE TOULOUSE-LAUTREC (Albi 1864–1901 Malromé)
La belle Hélène. Wash over pencil drawing. 620: 450 mm. Musée Toulouse-Lautrec, Albi.
Offenbach's operetta, *La belle Hélène*, received its first performance in November 1899, and was revived with enormous success in November 1900, with Cocyte in the title role. The singer is depicted here in all her Junoesque magnificence.

27 GEORGES ROUAULT (Paris 1871–1958)
In the Mirror. 1906. Watercolour on white card. 725:550 mm. Musée d'Art Moderne, Paris.
Rouault began to experiment with watercolours in 1902. He frequently used a blue underpainting, which creates a sombre, mysterious mood. His studies were 'not made to please', they are an indictment of coarseness and viciousness. He overemphasizes the flesh in this portrait of a prostitute, in order to reveal her true nature.

28 KARL SCHMIDT-ROTTLUFF (born Rottluff 1884)
The Artist and his wife. 1921. Watercolour. 600: 490 mm. Niedersächsische Landesgalerie, Hanover.
As he emerged from a cubist phase, Schmidt-Rottluff painted a series of self-portraits and double portraits of his wife and himself between 1919, the year of their marriage, and 1921.

29 WASSILY KANDINSKY (Moscow 1866–1944 Paris)
Head (*Composition in Blue, Green and Red*). Probably before 1920. Watercolour and body colour. 340: 226 mm. Albertina, Vienna. Inv. 23,492.
The discovery of the significance that lines, planes and colours could enjoy in their own right had the greatest consequences for art. For a long time, however, combinations of these elements continued to carry subjective associations, in this case a face. As elsewhere, Kandinsky is attempting to find 'the sound, that is, the soul of the form' appropriate to its appearance.

30 OSKAR KOKOSCHKA (born Pöchlarn 1886)
Standing Girl. Watercolour. 699:518 mm. Wallraf-Richartz-Museum, Cologne.
While he was in Dresden, from 1917 to 1924, Kokoschka discovered that the use of watercolour gave him an unparalleled facility in depicting the appearance and personality of his subjects.

31 FILIPPO DE PISIS (Ferrara 1896–1956 Milan)
Still-life with Pheasant. Watercolour. 260:410 mm. Galleria La Medusa, Rome.
Very few Italian artists of the twentieth century have pursued the nineteenth-century tradition of watercolour painting; among them, De Pisis stand out as an important innovator. In this *natura morta*, he uses a few, relaxed strokes of the brush and intense colours.

32 ZAO WOU-KI (born Peking 1920)
Ischia. 1953. Watercolour, pen in indian ink. 520:350 mm. Nesto Jacometti collection, Zurich.
A member of the École de Paris, this artist has lived in Paris since 1949, but his watercolours still reveal much of his oriental origins and his training in Hangchow under Lin Fong-Mien. Combining all the qualities of informal lyricism with an interpretative understanding of nature and landscape, they are among the most subtle of modern works in the medium.

25

26

27

28

29

30

31

32

pittura metafisica movement, all preferred other media, though Giorgio Morandi has continually used watercolour in landscapes and still-lifes, which convey an impression of calm and classic serenity. The style of Filippo de Pisis, another of the few contemporary Italian artists to work in watercolour, was strongly influenced by late impressionism; his composition involves a rhythmic marshalling of the surface, on which he sets out his subject with an austerity that is none the less lyrical (*pl. 31*).

Watercolour has become indispensable in its own right to artists of all levels of ability. It is not easy to select the most significant works from the vast quantity of material which ranges from some of the fairy-tale fantasies of Marc Chagall (*pl. XXI*) to the imposing compositions of Fernand Léger, the socio-political content of which could hardly be further removed from the products of Chagall's boundless imagination. Bernard Buffet, like Léger, has repeatedly used watercolour in pictures whose clear treatment of their subjects is primarily a matter of line. One of the most active of contemporary watercolourists is Zao Wou-ki. Born in Peking, he is a member of the École de Paris, and the finest of his lyrical, introspective works reveal a mutual interpenetration of the Far East and the West (*pl. 32*). A similar duality can be found in the sensitive works of the German Julius Bissier and the American Morris Graves, who have clearly been influenced by Far Eastern meditative philosophy. The German Ernst Wilhelm Nay also deserves special mention as an unquestioned master of the medium. His tightly organized abstract compositions employ all the special qualities of watercolour to particular advantage: luminosity, transparency and chromatic freshness in the play of complementary tensions.

The number of artists it is possible to name and the variety of trends they represent show that it will be a long time before the definitive history of watercolour in the twentieth century can be written. Wols (Wolfgang Schulze) is one who will occupy a key position in it for his creation of a truly new world, a microcosmic reflection of macrocosmic apprehensions. On the coast of the Mediterranean, at Cassis, he took a magnifying glass to his study of stones, fishes and rocks; arranging forms and colours by instinct, he found his way to a new beginning: '*Il faut savoir que tout rime*', everything rhymes, everything is united in an immense whole (*pl. XXIV*). Following a different path, Fritz Hundertwasser is working towards a similar end. He first began to paint in watercolour in 1954 while a patient in the Ospedale Santo Spirito in Rome and since then it has occupied an important position in his work. Trailing his characteristic spirals of jewel-like colours across the surface of all kinds of material including wrapping paper and envelopes, using various media, including coloured chalks, mixed media and egg tempera on polyvinyl grounds, he creates visual poems which are expressed in words in his titles.

In view of the current trends and the continuing popularity of watercolour, it is not possible to make secure predictions about its use in the future. This flexible medium has progressed from naturalistic depiction of landscape to the extremes of a-formality, but the next stage in its history can only be a matter of conjecture. Art is changing, as man himself is changing, in a world where changes follow one another with ever-increasing rapidity. The obsequies of watercolour have already been celebrated once, with the decline of impressionism at the turn of the century, and Brieger's monograph, which I have cited several times, ends with the valedictory: 'What watercolour strove for, what it fought for, has been achieved; there is nothing now for watercolour to do.' Yet watercolour had a great deal of new things to do, because of the changes in what artists wanted to achieve. We must beware of prophecy. Unless the world of the future, the new technocracy, the new rationalized human society, completely loses both the need for emotional expression and the urge to interpret the internal and external tensions and relationships which cannot be conveyed in any other way, art, and with it watercolour, will continue to serve an immemorial function.

XIX LYONEL FEININGER (New York 1871–1956).
Freighter I. 1924. Watercolour and pen and ink. 285:400 mm. Robert Norman Ketterer collection, Campione.
Feininger here abandons his crystalline fragmentation of urban views in order to depict atmospheric and thematic impressions. He continued to re-examine the themes of sea, sky, clouds and distant horizons in the numerous watercolours he painted after settling permanently in the United States in 1937.

Fracht-Dampfer I

Feininger   22 Juli 1924

XIX

XX

Painting with Watercolours

The watercolourist needs only the very simplest equipment familiar to every schoolchild: a paintbox with six or twelve colours in pots, tubes or cakes (six are sufficient for most needs); a block of good quality, hand-made paper; a medium-sized hair brush; a pot of water and a saucer; and finally a sponge (not synthetic), blotting paper and rags.

The paintbox should not only hold, store and protect the paints but should have shallow depressions in its lid in which colours can be thinned and mixed. A watercolour palette with several depressions serves the same purpose. When painting a larger, uniform surface, requiring a greater quantity of paint ready to hand, small tin vessels for each colour will be necessary. The order in which the colours should be placed on the palette should be carefully thought out in advance and should conform to some logical scheme such as warm to cold, light to dark, or follow the order of the colours in the rainbow.

Brushes The secret of successful brushwork in watercolour painting does not lie in using a large number of brushes of all sizes and types, but in the way the brush is handled, the amount of pressure and the kind of strokes made. A limitless quantity of dynamic variation is possible with even a single brush. Nevertheless, the choice of brush is a matter of some importance. The size will depend on the format of the paper to be used. On a medium-sized piece measuring about 12×20 in., brush Nos 6 to 8 will do, but No. 10 is better. The brush should be of the finest quality hair; the best is red sable, which is thick and bushy when dry, but runs to a fine point when wet. Brushes of polecat and bear hair have proved their worth in general use; dark, silky squirrel is especially soft and gives an extra-fine point. The stiffer brushes of hog bristle sometimes used in oil-painting are better for gouache. Since the brush must not be allowed to lose its elasticity, it should never be squashed or pressed out of shape. Brushes with flat or oval heads can be used for wetting the paper with clean water. It is also particularly important that the brush should always be absolutely clean before starting to paint, as a dirty brush will dim the brilliance of any colour.

Blotting paper and sponge Blotting paper is needed for drawing excess water off the brush, when the amount cannot be regulated by shaking. The amount of water on the brush determines the density, intensity and brilliance of the colour. If the paint that reaches the paper is still too liquid, the utmost care must be exercised in drawing off the excess with blotting paper; it is better to use the edge or corner, always absorbing the paint from the edge of the stain inward, unless you specifically desire the effect caused by pressing the blotting paper on the surface – a certain reduction in the transparency of the paint layer caused by particles of colour being pressed into the pores of the paper.

The sponge, too, can be used to absorb excess paint, but its principal function, for which it is almost indispensible, is to wet the paper all over before starting. It is also used to wipe out unsuccessful strokes, but this is only possible to a limited extent: watercolour can never be altered altogether, since the paper will never regain its original brightness.

The watercolourist's equipment is completed with waterpots, saucers and all the tins and tin lids he can lay his hands on.

Paper Ultimate success will be very largely determined by the choice of paper. The transparency of watercolours means that the whiteness of the paper plays an essential part, shining through the layers of paint and providing the highlights where it is left blank. It should be neither too large nor too small for convenience; not smaller than DIN A4, and the International format, 50 by 65 cm. (roughly 20× 25 in.), will probably be found quite large enough. The strength of a sheet is directly proportionate to its size; its weight should be somewhere between 90 and 140 lb. per ream of imperial sheets (between 180 and 300 grammes per square metre sheet).

The paper must be free of any wood pulp, since all cellulose papers are brittle and prone to turn yellow. Cotton-based papers take wet paint very badly. Hand-made linen papers are the only really suitable ones.

XX AUGUST MACKE (Meschede 1887–1914 Champagne).
In a yellow Jacket. 1913. Wash over faint pencil drawing. 290:440 mm. Städtische Sammlungen, Ulm.
Inspired by the metropolitan glitter of Berlin, the touch of modish elegance in Macke's work turns into a symbolic representation of the fleeting world of appearances.

The paper must also be sized throughout, not just on its surface, to ensure an absolutely even capacity for absorbing the paint; too much size will prevent absorption, too little will leave the paper too absorbent. Moreover, it should be completely free of alum, which makes colours run, and also of greasy substances, which hinder even absorption of the wet paint. The ash content, added to some papers to give them bulk, should not exceed 1 ½ per cent. Finally the paper must be bleached by natural means, since chemical bleaches, such as chloride of lime, can easily upset the sensitive pigments and alter the paper's whiteness.

The texture of the paper, which may vary from very smooth to rough and grainy, is a matter for individual taste but the choice will depend partly on the format of the sheet and beginners had best avoid either extreme. The surface texture will be found to affect the final appearance of the painting, but the most considerable effect of all will be that of the paper's natural colour. Paper for watercolour must be 'as white and clean as possible', as Max Doerner stipulates, and should tend to cream in preference to blue, as the latter has a tendency to make all colours appear cool.

Papers which possess all these qualities and enjoy an especially good reputation include, among white papers, Whatman paper made in England and Zanders-Bütten, Fabriano and Hahnemühle on the continent; among cream shades, Creswick, Joynson, Cartridge, Schöller-Hammer and Hardinge.

Paper has an unfortunate but quite unavoidable tendency to swell when it is wet, and this is more apparent with hand-made papers than with others. It can be ameliorated by painting as quickly as possible, but the longer the moisture has to soak in the worse the paper cockles, forming little valleys in which the paint collects. It helps to wet the paper all over on both sides before starting to paint, and to have it securely fixed to a drawing board or some other firm backing, such as a pad.

Paper that has been damaged in any way cannot be used for painting in watercolour: creases, scratches and the marks left by an eraser alter the surface and become immediately and ineradicably visible as soon as watercolours are laid over them.

Although pure watercolour or wash painting that depends principally on transparency for its effects always needs white paper, since this is the only backing that will shine through the colours as a permanent source of light, opaque water-soluble paints, such as gouache or tempera, will often benefit from a coloured ground, whether tinted paper or a tinted undercoat. The various stipulations made for white papers have little or no bearing on tinted papers. The colour of the ground can play a valuable part in the overall colour scheme in gouache and tempera painting, when the watercolour process is reversed and dark colours are painted first and highlights last.

Paints Unlike his predecessors, the modern painter does not need to make his own pigments from all manner of animal, vegetable and mineral ingredients, according to complicated recipes that were often jealously guarded secrets. Industrial and chemical research has made available a comprehensive range of high-quality soluble colours in all imaginable shades which have superseded some of the less durable of the older paints. It is therefore not necessary to enlarge upon the complex instructions for mixing colours found in old manuals, but it is interesting to note that as early as about 1410 Cennino Cennini wrote in his *Libro dell'Arte*: 'Know that there are seven natural colours, namely the four earths, black, red, yellow and green, and three other natural colours, which need to be prepared artificially: white,

XXI MARC CHAGALL (born Vitebsk 1889).
The Wounded Bird. Watercolour and body colour. 515:410 mm. Stedelijk Museum, Amsterdam.
In the twenties Chagall discovered in himself a close affinity to the animal creation. This picture with its profound sympathy for animal suffering dates from that period, one which Chagall has described as the happiest of his life.

XXII JOHN MARIN (Rutherford, New Jersey 1870–1953 Cape Split, Maine).
Town in Maine. 1932. Watercolour. 390:524 mm. Metropolitan Museum of Art, New York, Alfred Steiglitz Collection, 1949.
Marin's dynamic fragmentation of urban landscape became increasingly intense from 1910 on. But from 1931, the great elements of plasticity, colour and space are transformed, giving rise to extremely refined studies like this one.

XXI

XXII

XXIII

XXIV

blue and black.' He also speaks of 'certain paints which have no substance, which are called cloth colours and can be made with every colour'; by this he means all colours that can be transparent – in other words pure watercolours.

In practice, I would not recommend anyone to confine himself to the three primary colours, red, yellow and blue, although in strict theory they are all that is necessary, with perhaps the addition of black; on the other hand the beginner should resist the temptation to use as many of the available ready-made colours as he can. The following six basic shades will be found perfectly adequate:

1. *Cadmium yellow*   4. *Ultramarine blue*
2. *Cadmium red*   5. *Viridian*
3. *Madder lake*   6. *Ivory black*

The following twelve shades will give scope for greater richness and variety:

1. *Cadmium yellow*   7. *Cobalt blue*
2. *Cadmium orange*   8. *Ultramarine blue*
3. *Pale ochre*   9. *Prussian blue*
4. *Cadmium red*   10. *Viridian*
5. *Madder lake*   11. *Burnt umber*
6. *Burnt sienna*   12. *Black*

In addition to these two standard ranges (DIN A 5022 and A 5021) there are plenty of other colours, all of which have individual and very different qualities and which all entail specific advantages and disadvantages. The most important of these are:

White: Chinese white, Zinc white, Titanium.
Red: Terra di Siena (a brownish red of great luminosity), English red, *Caput mortuum*, Cinnabar (Vermilion), Saturn red, Geranium red, Rose madder.
Purple: Ultramarine violet, Cobalt violet.

Blue: Indigo, Parisian blue (sensitive to light).
Green: Terre verte, Paris green, Emerald green (poisonous).
Brown: Sepia, Raw umber.
Black: Blue black, Payne's Grey (a neutral grey).
Yellow: Yellow ochre, Indian yellow, Indanthrene yellow (instead of the poisonous Zinc yellow. Real Gamboge, too, is no longer used because of its impermanence).

Although it is no longer necessary for the artist to prepare his own colours, he ought to be familiar with the nature of his materials. An important component in any paint is the agent which binds the pigment, so that it does not simply rub off the paper when the water dries. In watercolours this is usually gum arabic, but tragacanth, dextrine and isinglass are also used, while admixtures of honey, candy, glycerine, syrup and gall prevent possible caking. In gouache the solvent manna, a resinous discharge of Sicilian and Calabrian ash trees, is used in addition to gum and white candy. Tempera is bound with egg yolk. The intensity of the binding agent is what makes the difference between gouache and watercolour; in the latter the pigment is bound in a fine colloid relationship and a greater proportion of the binding agent would cause the grains of pigment to clog together, resulting in opacity. Coarser grains of pigment, sometimes combined with opaque white, produce true body colour, or gouache, which makes a cohesive stain on the paper, whereas with watercolours fine grains dissolved in a transparent medium, stain by adhesion. Tempera is made by binding the grains of pigment in a kind of paste with an oil-based emulsion, which gives a harder consistency.

XXIII Wilhelm Thöny (Graz 1888–1949 New York).
Place de la Concorde, Paris. Watercolour. 510:675 mm. Trude Rendi collection, Graz.
Thöny, who lived in Paris from 1931, felt 'a great, romantic love' for the city, to which his watercolours bear witness. By about 1935 he had overcome the unease that oppressed him in the twenties and was able, as here, to express the essence of a moment in delicate, ethereal colours.

XXIV Wols (Wolfgang Schulze) (Berlin 1913–51 Paris).
The Bottle. 1950/51. Watercolour, gouache and pen and ink. 247:162 mm. Roché collection, Toulon.
Wols pioneered a completely new form of 'informal' painting. The lines and colours in this painting have an independent existence, each laid on spontaneously and impulsively. The artist's thematic intentions are ambiguous, but the painting is certainly more than a still-life.

The process of painting The technique of painting in watercolours is very simple and can be described in a few words, but it is not in itself of such importance as a certain subtle sensitivity combined with an aptitude which can be enhanced by practice but is not, ultimately, to be learned. Watercolour, apparently so simple, is perhaps in fact the most difficult of all artistic media.

Before starting, the artist must remind himself that corrections and erasures are virtually impossible in watercolour, and that all the important elements must therefore be quite clear in his mind from the outset: silhouette, composition and design, as well as the relative tonal values. Leonardo da Vinci's list of the ten things which the painter's eye must appraise before he begins is still valid: darkness, light, substance and colour, shape and position, distance and proximity, movement and repose.

The process is as follows. A sheet of suitable paper is secured to a firm support and is first of all moistened well all over, without being soaked to the extent that standing water cockles the surface. This stretches the paper a little, and as it starts to dry the construction of the picture can be sketched in, in very general outline, with not too soft a pencil (H will probably be found the best). The pencil lines will still be visible when the painting is finished, but rubbing-out must be avoided at all costs. The surface should then be wet all over again, preferably with soft or boiled water. When the paper is damp to just the right degree, the brush can make the first stroke. Always paint with a full brush and do not be afraid of either prodigality or speed. You must proceed quickly, because once a patch of colour has dried it has an edge which cannot be camouflaged by overpainting; therefore, as a general rule, it is best to eliminate unwanted edges by overpainting while the preceding wash is still wet.

It is very important to be able to alter the angle of the tilt of your paper; the tendency of the wet paint is to run downwards and collect with greatest intensity at the bottom, though if the brush is pressed out quickly, it can take up the excess before it dries. It is a good idea to make a few preliminary strokes on spare scraps of paper to test the density and strength of the paint.

Putting the colours directly on to the white paper in what is intended to be the final form is painting *alla prima,* and is the general practice nowadays. The earlier manner demanded an underpainting in a pale colour, which also had some advantages: the artist painted in the pale and neutral shades first and progressed towards the stronger shades, using the blank, white paper for highlights and leaving painted shadows and modelling until last. This is the classic method of watercolour, from light to dark tones. The modern method is to juxtapose tones in their full strength from the start; it is even permissible (and Doerner recommends it as practical) to start with shadows and progress towards highlights, which naturally have to be painted in opaque white body colour. 'In this, freshness is the all-important factor; overworked colour is dirty and dull.' On the other hand there is much to be said for Max Schmidt's advice to work as long as possible with half-tones and reserve the extremes of chromatic power for a few, carefully chosen areas. Too much dark energy will result, not in richness, but in blackness; just as the brightest lights must have a focus, so shadows must have a centre.

There is, however, plenty of scope for individual preference in approach. Max Schmidt, for instance, believed the first wash should already establish the main contrasts, the second should give everything in the painting its local colour, the third completely clarify the masses indicated in silhouette, and the fourth eliminate weaknesses and awkwardnesses. Colin Hayes recommends beginning with warm tones, since 'cool washes sit better on top of warm ones rather than vice versa.' Bodo Jaxtheimer, on the other hand, thinks it is better to start with cool colours, since these correspond to the tones of the background distances, while the warm tones of the foreground should be applied last: 'If you paint with the reverse procedure, the picture becomes heavy and without contrasts, which is especially unfortunate in a watercolour.'

There are three possible ways to combine two colours: overpainting a wash that has already dried, which creates the effect of glazing; mixing them in water on the palette or saucer to create a third colour; and overpainting a wet wash so that the colours merge on the paper. Which method is best in any particular circumstances, how best to deal with washes that are half dry, are things that can be learned from examples, the work of others, observation, experience and practice, but not from precepts.

Glossary

Additive colour see **Colour: mixing**

Body colours are those water-soluble paints which make an opaque stain on the painting surface, however thinly they are applied. The pigment is, strictly speaking, suspended in the water, not dissolved in it. The opacity also derives in part from the addition of white and other substances. Body colour always forms a layer of colour over, and distinct from, the surface of the paper, whereas watercolour always leaves the surface fully visible. (See also **Gouache**.)

Brilliance The brilliance of a colour is determined by its grey content, that is, the proportion of achromatic colour (black or white) in a chromatic colour (cf. **Colour: mixing** and **Complementary colours**). A high grey content gives a low brilliance, a small grey content gives intense brilliance.

Colour Light radiates from a source of energy. Colour is refracted light. The human eye is capable of receiving, registering and transmitting the impulses of a certain range of electro-magnetic waves, namely those between about 400 and 690 millionths of a millimetre, and each wavelength within this range represents a different colour. From the violets at the bottom of the spectrum, there is a continuous, fluid transition to the blues, then to greens, yellows, oranges and finally reds. Beyond each end of the spectrum are waves invisible to the human eye; the shorter being ultra-violet waves and the longer, infra-red waves. All these waves are bunched together and are invisible until the ray falls upon a body, when it becomes visible as white, or colourless light. Colourless light contains all the potentially visible wavelengths which can be made visible when the light is refracted. A surface or object only appears coloured because it absorbs a certain section of the spectrum, of the light falling on it, converts this into calorific energy and reflects the rest. The reflected section creates the impression of a colour. Colour is thus not a substance that rests on the surface of a body but the reflection of certain light waves, according to the character of the reflecting surface. Thus a red flower absorbs all the wavelengths of a ray of colourless light except the red ones; the eye receives the reflected red waves and transmits the stimulus 'red' to the brain. A green field reflects the 'green' wavelengths, a blue wall the 'blue' wavelengths. Bodies that absorb all wavelengths are black; bodies that reflect them all are white.

It follows that an object can only reflect those colours that are contained in the ray of light; a red light lacks any green waves, so a green object will appear black in a red light. This can be observed in nature, for instance in the red light of the setting sun, in twilight, which alters all colours, in moonlight etc.

Colour: memory Unlike colour film, which fixes an image with definite and unalterable chromatic relationships, by means of colour particles which are either contained in the film or laid over it, the retina of the human eye stores up chromatic impulses and relates them to chromatic impressions in a chain reaction. The relationship between colours determines, to a large extent, the effect that each one makes and this effect is, as a result, variable, not stable. This affects not only the warmth or coolness of a colour (the warmth of a green, for instance, depends on whether it is seen beside a cooler blue or a warmer orange), but also aesthetic qualities. If a particular shade dominates in a picture, it will determine its basic mood.

The process of variable relationships set in motion by the eye has far greater relevance to watercolour than to any opaque medium, if only because the light emanating from the white paper beneath the paint imperceptibly fluctuates all the time, so that the play of nuances is far less definite. By contrast the effect of surface light reflected by opaque colour is much more stable and physically defined, and this also determines its different surface character.

Colour: mixing There are two fundamentally different ways of mixing colours: additive and subtractive. The usual method of mixing pigments in solution or suspension is subtractive. A mixture of blue and yellow gives green by virtue of subtracting (or one might say, excluding) red, the third primary colour. The further this process of mixing by subtraction is taken, the darker the result; in theory a mixture of all colours gives black, the negation of the sum of all colours, white. In practice this means that every successive mixture of colours leads to a dimming of the chromatic intensity as it increasingly blackens. The artist in watercolours can avoid this in two ways: by the use of opaque white in *gouache-aquarelle*, and by mixing colours by the additive method of impressionism.

In theory additive mixing of colours by addition is possible only by mixing coloured light. However, in painting it is possible to juxtapose clear colours in such tiny spots that, at a certain distance, they give the impression of mixture without any blackening.

121

This is the principle that lies at the heart of pointillism, divisionism and neo-impressionism.

Colour: properties Every colour is determined by three traits: hue, saturation and brilliance. All colours, moreover, fall into one or other of two categories: chromatic and achromatic. Chromatic colours are those resulting from mixtures of the three primary colours or their derivatives; achromatic colours are the various tones of grey, from white to black.

Every colour has a certain 'temperature': cold colours are generally understood to be those ranging from alizarin red to ice blue, warm ones range from lime green to cadmium red. A whole science of colour psychology has grown out of the study of the quite specific perceptions which these properties arouse in the spectator. These perceptions include a phenomenon that has been called 'colour perspective': warm colours appear to come towards the spectator, while cold ones recede from the picture surface into the background. This tension between the colours on the surface is called chromatic space, and is one of the artist's basic means of formal creation. Colours also possess the property of summoning up in the spectator certain generally recognized associations and degrees of stimulation. This is based on the symbolism of common experience (sun – hot – orange) as well as on the instinctive foundations of human psychology (blood – life – red – aggressive). Every work of art containing colour exploits these common instinctive reactions and associations; accurate perception of them requires a natural sensitivity as well as practice, training and knowledge.

Three-dimensional space is created on a two-dimensional surface not by chromatic temperature alone, but by a number of other factors such as the lightness, density and form of the colours. A painting presents the spectator with the results of an exceedingly complex dynamic process and its full appreciation demands the greatest concentration and attentiveness in return.

Complementary colours are those pairs of colours which, if mixed, would contain equal proportions of all three preliminary colours (thus giving a neutral grey). Blue is complementary to orange (red and yellow), yellow to violet (blue and red) and red to green (blue and yellow). The closer two areas of colour come to being complementary, the greater the optical stimulation of their juxtaposition.

Gouache (from Italian *guazzo*, 'dew', because of the need to keep it moist) is an opaque paint in which the medium for suspending the pigment is water, not an emulsion. On the painting surface it has a substantial, 'dimensional' consistency. It is in fact the same as body colour. Tempera is opaque colour floated in various kinds of emulsion (such as egg-yolk).

Gouache-aquarelle is a technique employing transparent watercolours and body colours side by side. Areas of white are left blank and pale areas of colour are painted with a thin wash of watercolour, while areas of stronger colour are painted in body colour, with lighter shades being laid over darker ones.

Hue is the specific property (the wavelength) of a colour, by virtue of which it can be described as, for example red, yellow, violet, pink or blue.

Neutral colour The grey achieved by mixing complementary colours in equal proportions. Mixing white or black into chromatic colours dims their brilliance but does not neutralize them.

Pigment is the natural colouring material. It is ground into tiny particles and, together with a binding agent, is suspended or dissolved in a suitable fluid before being applied to the picture surface. Different densities and types of pigment produce different results. Watercolours contain very finely ground, almost transparent pigments dissolved in water, hence the transparency of a watercolour painting. Opaque pigments or an admixture of white create gouache or body colour, in which the actual substance of the suspended pigments is enough to form an opaque layer. Pigments bound with emulsions instead of water form tempera, which has a pulpy quality. Oil paint, though prepared in a completely different manner, is as thick as tempera, having an inherent physical substantiality, which can create an effect of plasticity when laid on the canvas heavily enough.

Primary colours Red, yellow and blue. All other colours can be obtained by mixtures of these.

Reflection is diffused light, both as it is reflected from a surface and as it falls on another object or on the eye; in the second sense it may be coloured. The effect that the colour of the reflected light will have on the colour of the object on which it falls depends on whether the object itself is lit or in shadow, and on whether the two colours tolerate each other or not. The intensities of hue, saturation and brilliance also play a part.

Saturation is a colour's vividness, increasing in inverse ratio to the grey content.

Secondary colours are those formed by mixing two primary colours; i.e. orange (from red and yellow), violet (from red and blue) and green (from blue and yellow).

Shadow can be defined as the area which an opaque body prevents light from penetrating. Two sources of light can each illuminate the shadow areas thrown by the other, in which case coloured lights will throw coloured shadows. It is by his handling of light, reflection, unlit areas, partly-lit areas and dense shadows that the artist creates on his surface the illusion of three-dimensional space and physical reality. A continuous shadow falling over several different shapes can be indicated by a continuous wash.

Subtractive colour see **Colour: mixing.**

Tertiary colours are those formed by mixing a colour with its complementary colour (*q.v.*) in such proportions that one of the primary colours is dominant: red in brown, yellow in ochre, blue in olive. If all the colours are equal in strength, the result will be grey (see **Neutral colour**).

Underpainting There are a number of different ways of preparing to paint a watercolour. Apart from a simple linear sketch, which will still be visible in the finished work, the tonal values can be mapped out in a neutral wash. A drawing already executed in pen and ink can be coloured in when dry, or it can

be painted while the ink is still wet, which will blur the definition of the lines. Alternatively, lines can be drawn with the pen either after the painting has been completed, to give clarity of definition to outlines if the paint is dry, or while the paint is still wet by deliberately exploiting the effect of the ink running.

Wash The painting of a large area in one colour with the brush, leaving the highlights blank. The tonal values of a piece can be roughed out in advance by a wash in a neutral shade. Interesting effects can be achieved by combining wash and other techniques, for instance using the brush to make a line, drawn with the pen, run while it is still wet.

Watercolour (French *aquarelle*). True, or pure, watercolour painting entails the use of transparent colours. Pale colours are applied first and then successive washes in progressively darker colours. The quality of each layer of colour is determined by the paler washes and ultimately by the white paper beneath, all of which are able to shine through the transparent overpainting. There are two ways in which light can illuminate a painting: by shining up out of the picture's own depths and by shining on to its surface. The luminescence of a watercolour painting depends very largely on the extent to which the refracted light which has passed through the coloured particles to the surface of the paper and is then reflected back through the colours again is stronger than the light reflected purely from the surface of the paint. This light from the depths of the painting is the essential difference between watercolours and body colours: the latter only reflect light from their surface and their character is therefore matt.

Bibliography

This list represents only a selection of the books and articles consulted by the author. All dictionaries and a large number of exhibition catalogues, have been omitted.

Amerikanische Meister des Aquarells, catalogue of an exhibition held at the Albertina, Vienna, 1949

H. Aulich, 'Aquarelltechnik in Verbindung mit Pigmenttuschen', in *Maltechnik LXIV*, 1958

G. Barret, *The Theory and Practice of Water Colour Painting*, London 1840

F. Beckert, *Die Aquarellmalerei und ihre Anwendung auf Architektur und Landschaft*, Strelitz 1923

E. Berger, *Die Technik des Aquarells und ihre Anwendung in Kunst und Kunstgewerbe* (second edition), Leipzig 1923

A. Biese, *Das Naturgefühl im Wandel der Zeiten*, Leipzig 1926

L. Binyon, *English Water-Colours* (second edition), London 1944

P.V. Bradshaw, *Watercolour, a Truly English Art*, London and New York 1952

L. Brieger, *Das Aquarell, seine Geschichte und seine Meister*, Berlin 1923

A.G. Bruckmann, *Albrecht Dürers Landschaftsaquarelle*, Berlin 1934

Bouchotte, *Les règles du dessin et du lavis pour les plans particuliers des ouvrages et des bâtiments*, Paris 1743

A. Bury, *Watercolour Painting of Today* (special number of *The Studio*), London 1937

G. Busch, *Die Tunisreise, Aquarelle und Zeichnungen von August Macke*, Cologne 1958

A. Cassagne, *Traité d'Aquarelles* (second edition), Paris 1886

A.M. Cetto, *Watercolours by Albrecht Dürer*, New York and Basle 1954

R. Cogniat, *XXth Century Drawings and Watercolours*, Milan 1966

W.G. Constable, *Richard Wilson*, London 1953

S.F. Constant-Viguier, *Manuel de miniature et de gouache … suivi du Manuel du lavis à la sépia et de l'aquarelle, par F.P. Langlois de Longueville* (Encyclopédie Roret), Paris 1828

H.M. Cundall, *A History of British Water Colour Painting*, London 1908

Deutsche und französische Aquarelle und Zeichnungen 1870–1930, catalogue of an exhibition held at the Staatliche Graphische Sammlung, Munich, 1968

M. Doerner, *The Materials of the Artist and their Use in Painting*, London 1935

D. Duville, *La Gouache*, Paris 1946

Englische Aquarelle des 18. Jahrhunderts, catalogue of an exhibition held at the Albertina, Vienna, 1965

English Drawings from the Whitworth Art Gallery, catalogue of an exhibition held at the University of Manchester, 1967

A.J. Finberg, *Early English Water-Colour Drawings by the Great Masters* (special number of *The Studio*), London 1919

A.J. Finberg, *The English Water Colour Painters*, London 1906

L.H. Fischer, *Die Technik der Aquarellmalerei*, Vienna 1901

A.T.E. Gardner, *A History of Watercolor Painting in America*, New York 1966

H. Gasser, *Techniques of Painting*, New York 1958

K. Gerstenberg, *Claude Lorrain*, Baden-Baden 1952

E.H. Gombrich, *Norm and Form: Studies in the Art of the Renaissance*, London 1966

O. Götz, *Dürers Landschaftsaquarelle*, Leipzig 1925

L. Gowing, *Turner: Imagination and Reality* (Museum of Modern Art), New York 1966

E. Gradmann, 'Das englische Aquarell' in *Festschrift Hahnloser*, Basle 1961

M.H. Grant, *A Dictionary of British Landscape Painters*, Leigh-on-Sea 1952

B. Haencke, *Die Chronologie der Landschaften Albrecht Dürers* (Studien zur deutschen Kunstgeschichte), Strasbourg 1899

W. Haftmann, *Master Watercolours of the Twentieth Century*, New York 1965

M. Hardie, *Water-colour Painting in Britain*: Vol. I: *The Eighteenth Century*; Vol. II: *The Romantic Period*, London 1967

C. Hayes, *The Technique of Water-colour Painting*, London and New York 1967

J. Hayes, 'British Patrons and Landscape Painting', four articles in *Apollo*, 1965–67

K. Herberts, *The Complete Book of Artists' Techniques*, London 1958

A. Hickethier, *Einmaleins der Farbe*, Ravensburg 1963

A.M. Hind, 'A Landscape Drawing attributed to Van Dyck', in *British Museum Quarterly*, 7, 1932–33

W. Hofmann, *Expressionist Watercolors, 1905–20*, New York 1967

R. Huyghe and P. Jaccottet, *French Drawing of the 19th century*, London and New York 1956

F. Jaennicke, *Handbuch der Aquarellmalerei* eighth edition (revised by F.S. Meyer), Esslingen 1920

B.W. Jaxtheimer, *How to Paint and Draw*, London 1962

L. Klebs, 'Dürers Landschaften' in *Repertorium für Kunstwissenschaft*, XXX, 1907

P. Klee, *The Inward Vision: Watercolours, Drawings, Writings*, London 1958

W. Koschatzky, *Meisterwerke des Klassizismus*, catalogue of an exhibition held at Graz, 1961

W. Koschatzky, *Thomas Ender, Zeichnungen und Aquarelle*, catalogue of an exhibition held at the Albertina, Vienna, 1964

F. Landsberger, *Die Kunst der Goethezeit*, Leipzig 1931

H. Lemaitre, *Le paysage anglais à l'aquarelle, 1760–1851*, Paris 1955

H. Leporini, 'Aquarell' in *Reallexikon zur deutschen Kunstgeschichte* (Vol. I), Stuttgart 1937

H.H. Leuner, *Das Aquarell*, Dresden 1959

F. Lippmann, *Zeichnungen von Albrecht Dürer*, Berlin 1905–27

M. Lüscher, *Psychologie der Farben*, Basle n.d.

J.A. Macintyre and H. Buckley, 'The Fading of Water-colour Pictures', in *The Burlington Magazine*, LVII, 1930

E.W. Manwaring, *Italian Landscape in Eighteenth Century England*, New York 1925

R. Mayer, *The Artist's Handbook of Materials and Techniques* (second edition), London and New York 1964

A. Mende, 'Gegen das Wellen des Aquarellpapiers', in *Maltechnik*, LXX, 1964

Moderne englische Graphik und Aquarellkunst, catalogue of an exhibition held at the Albertina, Vienna, 1948

G.E. Müller, *Über die Farben-Empfindungen* (Vol. 2), Leipzig 1930

A. Neumeyer, *Cézanne, drawings*, New York 1958, London 1959

F. Nocker, *Aquarellmalerei* (thirteenth edition), Ravensburg 1964

H.V.S. Ogden, *English Taste in Landscape in the Seventeenth Century*, Ann Arbor 1955

E. Panofsky, *Albrecht Dürer* (2 vols), London 1945

E. Panofsky, *Dürers Kunsttheorie*, Berlin 1915

D. Pataky, *Hungarian Drawings and Water-Colours*, Budapest 1961

H. Platte, *Die Maler des großen Lichts*, Brunswick 1967

P.O. Rave, *Karl Blechen, Leben, Werk, Würdigung* (Deutscher Verein für Kunstwissenschaft), Berlin 1940

L. Réau, *Un siècle d'aquarelle de Géricault à nos jours*, catalogue of an exhibition held at the Galerie Charpentier, Paris, 1942

G. Redgrave, *A History of Water-Colour Painting in England*, London 1892

G. Reynolds, *An Introduction to English Water-Colour Painting*, London and New York 1950

G. Reynolds, *Catalogue of the Constable Collection* (Victoria and Albert Museum), London 1960

S. Ricci, *L'aquarelle nella grande arte italiana*, Milan 1913

A. Roessler, *Rudolf von Alt*, Vienna 1921

J.L. Roget, *A History of the 'Old Water-Colour Society'* (2 vols), London 1891

Romantic Art in Britain, catalogue of an exhibition held at the Detroit Institute of Arts, 1968

E. Schilling, *Albrecht Dürer, Drawings and Water-colours*, London 1949

M. Schmid, *Die Aquarellmalerei: Technik derselben in Anwendung auf die Landschaftsmalerei*, Leipzig 1901

M. Schmidt, *Bemerkungen über die Technik der Aquarell-Malerei in ihrer Anwendung auf die Landschafts-Malerei* (sixth edition), Leipzig 1890

P.F. Schmidt, *Deutsche Landschaftsmalerei von 1750–1830*, Munich 1922

A. Schrödter, *Schule der Aquarellmalerei*, Bremen 1871

H. Schwarz, *Salzburg und das Salzkammergut*, Vienna 1926

G. Sheringham, *British Watercolour Painting of Today* (special number of *The Studio*), London 1921

G. Sheringham, *Figure Painting in Watercolour* (special number of *The Studio*), London 1923

O. Stelzer, *Die Vorgeschichte der abstrakten Kunst*, Munich 1964

M. von Thausing, *Albrecht Dürer, his life and works* (2 vols), London, 1882

H. Tietze, *Dürer als Zeichner und Aquarellist*, Vienna 1951

H. Tietze and E. Tietze-Conrat, *Kritisches Verzeichnis der Werke Albrecht Dürers* (3 vols), Augsburg, Basle and Leipzig 1928–38

M. Urban, *Emil Nolde, Blumen und Tiere. Aquarelle und Zeichnungen*, Cologne 1965

E.K. Waterhouse, *Painting in Britain, 1530–1790*, London 1953

K. Wehlte, *Malen mit Wasserfarben*, Ravensburg 1964

K. Wehlte, *Werkstoffe und Technik der Malerei*, Ravensburg 1967

I.A. Williams, *Early English Watercolours*, London 1952

F. Winkler, *Albrecht Dürer, Leben und Werk*, Berlin 1957

H. Wölfflin, *Die Kunst Albrecht Dürers*, Munich 1905

Index

Figures in italics refer to illustrations, roman numerals refer to colour plates

Acknowledgments

The reproductions were made with the kind permission of the museums, galleries and collections named in the captions or of the artists or their agents. The illustrations are taken frome the following photographic agencies, museums and archives: Albertina, Vienna: *Pls VIII, IX, X, XXIII, 2, 7, 14, 15, 16, 18, 22, 29*; Boymans-Van Beuningen Museum, Rotterdam: *Pl. 6*; British Museum, London: *Pls VI, VII, 3*; Brückmann-Verlag, Munich: *Pl. XIX*; J.E. Bulloz, Paris: *Pl. XII*; City Art Gallery, Birmingham: *Pl. 10*; Devonshire Collection, Chatsworth (Zoltan Weger, London): *Pl. I*; Fogg Art Museum, Cambridge, Mass.: *Pl. 21*; Galleria La Medusa, Rome: *Pl. 31*; Ganymed Press London Ltd, London: *Pls II, IV*; Erich S. Herma, New York: *Pl. XXII*; Nesto Jacometti, Locarno: *Pl. 32*; Photo Liberté, Toulon, *Pl. XXIV*; Musée National du Louvre, Paris: *Pls III, XI, XIII, 1*; Musée d'Albi: *Pl. 26*; Museum der Stadt Ulm: *Pls XVI, XX*; Niedersächsische Landesgalerie, Hanover: *Pl. 28*; C.L.T. Oppé, London: *Pl. 8*; Philadelphia Museum of Art, Philadelphia: *Pl. 25*; Rheinisches Bildarchiv, Cologne: *Pl. 30*; Schroll-Archiv, Vienna: *Pls IV, X, XIV, 4, 5, 12, 13, 24*; Service de Documentation photographique des Musées Nationaux, Paris: *Pl. 27*; Staatliche Graphische Sammlung, Munich: *Pl. 19*; Staatliche Kunsthalle, Karlsruhe: *Pls 17, 20*; Staatliche Kunstsammlung, Weimar: *Pl. XV*; Staatliche Museen zu Berlin, Nationalgalerie, Berlin: *Pl. 23*; Stedelijk Museum, Amsterdam: *Pl. XXI*; Stiftung Ada und Emil Nolde, Neunkirchen/Niebüll: *Pl. XVII*; Tate Gallery, London: *Pl. 9*; Victoria and Albert Museum, London: *Pl. 11*; Yale University Art Gallery, New Haven: *Pl. XVIII*.